Blush

FACES OF SHAME

Elspeth Probyn

University of Minnesota Press

Minneapolis — London

"Some Like Indians Endure," by Paula Gunn Allen, reprinted with permission of the poet.

Published by the University of Minnesota Press
111 Third Avenue South, Suite 290
Minneapolis, MN 55401-2520
http://www.upress.umn.edu

Library of Congress Cataloging-in-Publication Data

Probyn, Elspeth, 1958–
    Blush : faces of shame / Elspeth Probyn.
        p. cm.
    Includes bibliographical references and index.
    ISBN 0-8166-2720-7 (hc : alk. paper) — ISBN 0-8166-2721-5
(pbk. : alk. paper)
    1. Shame.   I. Title.
    BF575.S45P76 2005
    152.4'4—dc22
                                        2004023858
    PRO

Printed in the United States of America on acid-free paper

The University of Minnesota is an equal-opportunity educator and employer.

12 11 10 09 08 07 06 05   10 9 8 7 6 5 4 3 2 1

Contents

Acknowledgments

So MANY PEOPLE HAVE HELPED THIS BOOK come into being. For their engagement with the ideas as they progressed, I'd like to thank Margaret Buchanan, Jack Durack, Adam Eldridge, Anna Gibbs, Natalya Lusty, Gail Mason, Jeannie Martin, Rosemary Pringle, and Mandy Thomas.

I was fortunate to be invited to teach and present the central themes of the book. My time as a Noted Scholar in the Department of English at the University of British Columbia was formative, and I thank Sneja Gunew and especially the graduate students with whom I discussed ideas about affect. My thanks also to Rosi Braidotti and to the students who attended the master class on affect that I gave in the Women's Studies Institute at the University of Utrecht. Invitations to the Institute of Women's Studies at Lancaster University have been important to the development of my thinking, and my thanks to Jackie Stacey and Sara Ahmed as well as seminar participants. Bev Skegss, Lisa Adkins, and Nicole Vitteloni at the University of Manchester challenged me to reconsider the importance of Pierre Bourdieu. The Transculturalisms symposiums organized by Sneja Gunew and Ann Kaplan have been inspiring, and I also thank the Rockefeller Foundation for the time at the Bellagio Center. My study leave in the Department of Sociology at the London School of Economics was formative; my warm thanks to Nikolas Rose. The Australian

Research Council provided funding, and the Australian Academy with the Royal Academy of the Netherlands provided for my visit to Utrecht. My fondest thanks to my colleagues and students in the Department of Gender Studies at the University of Sydney. Special thanks to Michael Moller, Cathy Perkins, Melissa Gregg, and Gilbert Caluya for their help in editing.

I have written that shame is painful to write about, and I want to thank all those who helped at different moments, including Wendy Brady, Robyn and Jack Durack, Jon Hird, Alan Inglis, Rosemary Pringle, Jane Probyn, and Zoe Sofoulis. My family's pride in my work is tremendously important, and I especially thank my father.

Finally, to Sarah Donald, for making me shamelessly happy.

Introduction

Shame in Love

W HEN YOU GET VERY INTERESTED in something, it quickly seems that the whole world is revealed in its light. Falling in love is a good example. As I was writing this book, a phrase echoed in my brain like a pesky tune: "shame in love." It's ambiguous; it could refer to the shame that attends being in love or to being in love with shame. Of course, being in love offers endless possibilities for shame. But I've also been uneasily in love with the idea of shame. It's an uneasy affair, because shame is not usually thought of in a positive light. It's like falling for a seemingly reprehensible person and having to convince your friends that the loved one has hidden merits. Along the same lines, I want everyone to understand that shame is interesting and important: we cannot live without it, nor should we try.

I've fallen hard for some of the ideas about shame that I convey in this book. The compelling notion of shame's productive role I take from the American psychologist Silvan Tomkins (1911–1991). In the 1950s and 1960s, Tomkins elaborated a complex set of ideas about shame and other affects, such as joy, anger, disgust, and contempt. From Tomkins I take the initially startling idea that interest and shame are intimately connected. Shame, he argues, "operates only after interest or enjoyment has been activated."[1] Once you think about it, this becomes obvious. Only something or someone that has interested you can produce a flush of shame. Someone looks at you with interest and you begin to be interested, only to realize she's looking at someone else. Or, as Tomkins notes, "One started to smile but found one was smiling at a stranger."[2] If you're interested in and care about the interest of others, you spend much of your life blushing. Conversely, if you don't care, then attempts to shame won't move you. Shame highlights different levels of interest. Shame goes to the heart of who we think we are. In this sense, shame puts one's self-esteem on the line and questions our value system. The things that make me ashamed have to do with a strong interest in being a good person. What that means is normally quite nebulous, but once I've felt that hot blush, I'm reminded of what it is that I hold dear—not hurting people unnecessarily, being generous in my ideas and care for others, and so on. My list will be different from yours. What shames me may not shame you. But whatever it is that shames you will be something important to you, an essential part of yourself.

What makes shame remarkable is that it reveals with precision our values, hopes, and aspirations, beyond the generalities of good manners and cultural norms. For instance, sexuality is widely held as an area ripe for shame. But it's not a site of shame, or not the same site of shame, for everyone. I don't think I've ever been shamed for not being a heterosexual, but I have been shamed for not being a good homosexual. In other words, banal things that are supposed to make us ashamed quite often don't. And those things that do make us ashamed often reveal deep worries and concerns. Again, interest is the key to understanding shame, and shame reminds us with urgency what we are interested in. Shame reminds us about the promises we keep to ourselves.

Interest involves a desire for connection. At a basic level, it has to do with our longing for communication, touch, lines of entanglement, and reciprocity. Listen to this passage from Tomkins:

If you like to be kissed and I like to kiss you, we may enjoy each other. If you like to be sucked and bitten and I like to suck or bite you, we may enjoy each other. If you like to have your skin rubbed and I like to do this to you, we can enjoy each other. If you enjoy being hugged and I like to hug you, it can be mutually enjoyable. . . . If you enjoy communicating your experiences and ideas and aspirations and I enjoy being informed about the experiences, ideas and aspirations of others, we can enjoy each other.[3]

The cadence of the writing bathes the reader in a warm bath of love reciprocated. At the same time, it conjures up the terror of love and interest not being mutual. The wording captures the knife edge of falling in love: "we *can* enjoy each other" jostles with "we *may* enjoy each other." Interest is always hedged by the conditional *if.* That *if* contains the seeds for shame. Tomkins follows with a description that speaks of what happens when interest or love falters:

You may crave much body contact and silent communion and I wish to talk. You wish to stare deeply into my eyes, but I achieve intimacy only in the dark in sexual embrace. You wish to be fed and cared for, and I wish to exhibit myself and be looked at. You wish to be hugged and to have your skin rubbed, and I wish to reveal myself only by discussing my philosophy of life. . . . You wish to communicate your most personal feelings about me, but I can achieve social intimacy only through a commonly shared opinion about the merits of something quite impersonal, such as a particular theory or branch of knowledge or an automobile.[4]

The acuity of this description is painful. It is not the big bang catastrophe of falling out of love, but the harder, perhaps more mature, and deeply shaming experience of an incompatibility between two people. The bonds of interest slip: you wish to be cared for, and I talk about theory; I wish to be hugged, and you talk about yourself; you wish for silent communion, and I need promises of love. Not quite in love enough but enough in love to hope; interest is interrupted. The rupture is painful: "what could have been" is such a sad and shameful refrain.

Tomkins describes how shame can appear only once interest and enjoyment have been felt and when they have been ripped from you. At that moment the sheer disappointment of loss translates into shame that attacks your sense of self: the entrails of who you thought you were are suddenly displayed for all to judge. In Tomkins's description:

> The innate activator of shame is the incomplete reduction
> of interest or joy. Hence any barrier to further exploration
> which partially reduces interest . . . will activate the lowering
> of the head and the eyes in shame and reduce further explo-
> ration or self-exposure.[5]

Tomkins's insistence that shame flags the incomplete reduction of interest and joy is a crucial insight that propels my own argument. It describes shame as an ambiguous state of feeling, emotion, and affect. It gestures to shame as the fine line or border between moving forward into more interest or falling back into humiliation.

While some will find that the ideas I cite resonate deeply, others might find it hard to fathom why shame should be considered productive. On a basic level, shame always produces effects—small and large, individual and collective. Shame demands acknowledgment. As we blush, we are made visible at the very moment we want to cover our faces and hide. But, equally, shame compels an involuntary and immediate reassessment of ourselves: Why am I ashamed? Why did I say or do that? Can I rectify the actions that have either brought shame upon myself or caused someone else's shame? Shame in this way is positive in its self-evaluative role; it can even be self-transforming. This is possible, however, only where shame is acknowledged. Denying or eradicating shame, whether by an individual or a community, seems futile to me. It is also a waste of an important resource in thinking about what it means to be human.

Shame is a fact of human life. In many societies and cultures it is used to manage human social interaction. In others, it is hidden away: "corrected" in self-help programs and denied by governments wary of apologizing for past wrongs. Shame is very important right now: to discussions and debates about how to deal with pasts that could be called shameful; and to visions of life curtailed by the idea that there is something intrinsically wrong with feeling shame.

That shame is seen as deeply shameful has important implications for what we, as individuals and as a collectivity, can do with it. My argument seeks to investigate why it is considered shaming to admit to shame. After all, people freely admit to other negative affects, such as anger, which can lead to violence. In comparison, admitting shame is much more likely to spur consideration of why one feels ashamed. Shame, it is argued, can entail self-evaluation and transformation. To consider shame is not to wallow in self-pity or in the resentment that accompanies guilt. It is to recognize that the reduction of interest that prompts shame is always incomplete. As such, shame promises a return of interest, joy, and connection. This is why shame matters to individuals. And it is why studies of shame are important.

Over the course of this book I explore some of the immense variety of experiences, expressions, and thoughts about shame. These ideas often concern questions about humanness, humanity, and humility. I am taken by the argument that shame is biologically innate—that we are all born with the capacity for shame. While in some circles this essentialism may be considered heretical, it seems to me that we miss a great deal when we disregard our human similarities. In terms of how we feel physiologically, we are much more alike than different—whatever the measure of difference: gender, race, ethnicity, sexuality, and so on. This is not to say that we all experience shame in the same way or that some will not be more vulnerable to shame. I will experience shame differently from an Aboriginal man. But surely that does not annul our shared capacity for feeling it. To paraphrase Sojourner Truth: prick me, do I not bleed; shame me, do I not blush? When we deny shame or ignore it, we lose a crucial opportunity to reflect on what makes us different and the same.

Shame gives us a way to rethink the types of oppositions that have become entrenched in popular debate. If, as many have argued, pride is acceptable and even vaunted, surely we must also acknowledge our individual and collective shame. This should involve more than merely accepting shame in national and cultural narratives. We must use shame to re-evaluate how we are positioned in relation to the past and to rethink how we wish to live in proximity to others.

In *Blush,* I explore the conceptual resources shame can offer. Different disciplines have thought about shame in varied ways. On the more scientific side of psychology, shame tells us something about how our bodies dictate what we feel. In anthropology and sociology, studies of shame provide fascinating glimpses into quite different ways of managing social life. One of the abiding arguments in this book is that we need to be more open to ideas that seem beyond our intellectual comfort zone. Rather than dismissing or ignoring ideas about biology, psychology, and the innate nature of shame, let's see what these ideas do. This is not to say that arguments about the physiology of shame are any truer than those about its cultural expressions; it is to ask how very different ideas might mutually inflect and extend what we know.

This book is not a dissertation; it is an invitation to come exploring with me and to discover sidetracks of your own. There are stories and more stories—some of them mine, others that I retell from academic and literary sources. The emphasis on narrative is important when you're dealing with new ideas and new ways of being. With something as sensitive as shame, it's foolhardy to weigh in with ready-made theories or pronouncements. So I try not to. My stories are told in the spirit of experimentation: wouldn't it be interesting if we could all talk about shame in more productive ways?

The chapters build on one another. In the first I introduce some basic ideas about shame and begin to outline my case for why shame is interesting. I want you to see shame from different perspectives, to hear how the body in shame can be described. Some of the descriptions I include of shame as innate, essential, biological, universal are put in such interesting ways that they caused my previous prejudice to come undone. Interest may be of great use in undoing the fear, anxiety, suspicion, and at times loathing that can greet any description that comes to us from an unfamiliar realm.

Whether shame is an emotion or an affect is a point that divides much research. In general, the humanities and social sciences lean toward emotion, and the sciences tend to privilege affect. In other terms, and as another rough way of understanding the division, those interested in cognition, social expression, and the interpretation of cultures tend to study emotions. Those interested in the workings of the brain and the body study affects or the affect system. Very few writers cross the divide between the social and the biological. More often than not, one camp ignores the other. Rejecting the possibility that there are biological, neurological, and, more generally, bodily aspects of shame is as reductive as bald statements that ignore the cultural context in which affects are expressed and used within societies.

In the second chapter, driven by the ways in which Tomkins and others make me think about the body, I narrate a moment of shame I felt when I first experienced the awesome power of Uluru. Coming across the sight of that monument of nature and of Australian Aboriginal culture, I was physically struck by a variant of shame I call the shame of being out-of-place. This is the feeling the body registers in social and cultural contexts when it doesn't belong. When you feel like a fish out of water, your body reacts in shame. I draw on the French sociologist Pierre Bourdieu's thoughts about habitus, a term he uses to describe how we embody history. The body is a repository for the social and cultural rules that, consciously or not, we take on. Our bodies can also tell us when we have stumbled into other people's history, culture, and beliefs of which we are ignorant. Through my own story and those of others, I explore how the shame of being out-of-place can ignite a desire for connection. In the Australian context, that desire is called Reconciliation. It is an inspiration for modes of coexistence between non-Indigenous and Indigenous that can succeed only if we acknowledge different types of shame and interest.

The third chapter follows the passage of shame from the body into the body politic. While shaming people is a powerful and potentially destructive and violent way to patrol the borders of normality, in some societies it has been used to good effect to manage antisocial behavior. It all depends on the structure of the society and how it uses shaming. John Braithwaite, who has made shaming an important topic within criminology, bases his theory on a Maori tradition of shaming members of a community who break its rules. His ideas about reintegrative shaming have influenced policy in several contexts. Some of these are questionable, for example, a U.S. jurisdiction where drunk drivers are made to wear sandwich boards announcing themselves as such. Does shaming as a tactic for punishment and deterrence work in a Western context, where community bonds are not the norm and there is often little desire to be reintegrated into a community?

This question and related ones demand precise and grounded studies, which are beyond the scope of this book. However, Braithwaite's ideas spark thoughts about forms of shaming:

who is shamed and who is the shamer? I use them to consider
how in popular perception feminism has taken the moral high
ground in order to shame men and sometimes women. It's a
rude critique, but I stand by the argument that any politics not
interested in those it sees as outside its ken will ultimately fail
to interest and engage.

"Ancestral Shame," the fourth chapter, follows through on
arguments about shame and proximity. I turn to the notion
of the contact zone as the space where people and ideas are
brought together, often with powerfully emotional results. I
explore the types of shame that circulate within contact zones
to produce what might be called an intimate history of shame.
Addressing my own ancestral shame, I examine a poem by my
grandmother, titled "Half Breed," and ask whether it can be
mined for a more sympathetic analysis of individuals within
postcolonial contact zones.

The last chapter, "Writing Shame," raises the question of
a shame-based ethics of writing. My argument is that a form
of shame always attends the writer. Primarily it is the shame
of not being equal to the interest of one's subject. Drawing
on examples taken from a range of writers—Stephen King,
Gilles Deleuze, and Primo Levi—I elaborate on the different
ways they tell us about the seriousness of writing, how writing shame radically rearranges bodies, and the precision and
passion that constitute honest writing. It seems to me that
sometimes cultural theory gets carried away, forgetting that
theories and theoretical writing are of interest for what they
can do, what they let us understand, and what they make us
question.

One of the more frustrating aspects of reading across studies
of emotion and affect is the tendency to speak in general terms.
The various emotions and affects are distinct: each makes us
feel different and has quite specific effects in society. They demand precise description. One of the reasons we are afraid of
shame is that it tends to be paired in limiting ways: shame and

pride, shame and guilt. The relationship between the terms is seen as one of either opposition or mutual exclusivity, for example, where shame necessarily detracts from pride. My claim, backed by the findings of others, is that shame is positive. This should not be understood as yet another celebratory account of transgression. Shame is not subversive. Shame just *is*. How it is experienced and theorized varies, but nonetheless it is a fact of human life. It is productive in how it makes us think again about bodies, societies, and human interaction. That shame is both universal and particular, universalizing and particularizing, should be a resource, not a point of division. Shame raises questions of great and enduring interest concerning what it means to be human. Shame also demands that big questions be asked in a modest way.

This is perhaps the most personal book I've written and also the most objective. I had to write this book. Shame and its interests got under my skin.[6] Just as I have been engaged by and interested in the research and writers I talk about, I hope that some of the lines thrown out by this book will catch and set off more interest. It's a hope that I am trying to be shameless about.

1

Doing Shame

MOMENTS OF SHAME: An e-mail arrives from a respected colleague. She's angry at a newspaper column
I've written. She writes: "Loyalty? Shame? Irony?" In front
of my computer and a hemisphere away from her, I blush.
Thoughts of denial flit across my mind but are pushed away
by the visceral feeling of having done wrong. What can I say
but that I'm sorry? It seems such a paltry word compared with
the shame that covers me. And I don't say it. Or at least not
immediately. I waffle in reply about how I shouldn't think out
loud in print.

Another moment returns with a blush, and I am back in
time. I've made a girl cry. We must have been about eight years
old. I tease her about not having the same name as her mother.
She starts crying, and the nuns at the school chastise me. I'm
ashamed, even without knowing what I've done. I couldn't
have known that when her mother remarried she'd taken another man's name. The ignorance doesn't stop me from blushing. Now I feel a deeper shame at the thought of that little girl
crying from the pain of her parents' divorce.

Why is it that the mere recollection of a shameful moment
can cause you to blush? Distanced in years, an incident from
childhood returns with intensity, and one relives that horrible
feeling. As Kim Scott writes, "Bury memory deep in shame."[1]
Equally, the shame buried in memory seems to erupt, having

lost none of its sharp pain. And you blush, the only feeling that physically covers the face. In French, one blushes to the whites of the eyes, to the ears, and to the roots of one's hair. The tentacles of the blush, of blood rushing to the face, attest to the inner cringe.

Blushing feels bad, and it's a reaction that cannot be faked or brought on without experiencing or remembering the feeling of shame. Shame makes us feel small and somehow undone. It's no wonder that in most societies, shame tends not to be talked about, let alone vaunted. Other negative emotions, such as anger or rage or guilt or sadness, are regularly discussed in both popular and academic accounts. But shame makes an appearance only in discussions about pride, and then only as a shameful feeling. National pride, black pride, gay pride, and now fat pride are all projects premised on the eradication of shame. As political projects, they clearly, and often with very good reasons, denounce shame. Increasingly, there is a sense that pride is an entitlement, a state we will all achieve once we have overcome our nagging feelings of shame and once society becomes a place where no one shames another.

It's hard not to concur with such hopes—to aspire to live with only "good" and pleasurable emotions. There is nothing pleasurable about shame, but there is something immensely interesting about it in all its expressions. Certainly, compared with guilt, shame constitutes an acute state of sensitivity. Guilt is easier to get rid of and once dealt with is forgotten, whereas shame lingers deep within the self. Being shamed is not unlike being in love. The blush resonates with the first flush of desire. It carries the uncertainty about oneself and about the object of love; the world is revealed anew and the skin feels raw. Shame makes us quiver. In his psychoanalytic investigation of shame, Gerhart Piers cites this remarkable passage from Hegel:

> Shame does not mean to be ashamed of loving, say on account of exposing or surrendering the body . . . but to be

ashamed that love is not complete, that . . . there [is] something inimical in oneself which keeps love from reaching
completion.

Piers follows with the observation that

behind the feeling of shame stands not the fear of hatred,
but the fear of *contempt* which, on an even deeper level of
the unconscious, spells fear of *abandonment,* the death by
emotional starvation.[2]

These descriptions brutally expose the significance of
shame. Shame emerges as a kind of primal reaction to the
very possibility of love—either of oneself or of another. The
fear of contempt and abandonment is experienced as intensely
personal, but it can be seen at a societal level. For many, shame
is understood as "a sickness of the self." In Hegel's words, we
hear the anguish of not loving enough, of not being lovable.
For Piers, the immensity of the social comes crashing through.
Shame brings the fear of abandonment by society, of being left
to starve outside the boundaries of humankind. In these descriptions, it is a capacity for shame that makes us such fragile
beings. Hegel and Piers suggest that shame may provide a key
to the question that is now again gaining urgency: what is it
to be human?[3]

From there, and before we can even get to that question,
many others need to be asked: How do we feel shame? How
do we know it? What can we do with the feelings and the
knowledge that shame brings? These are some of the questions
that drive this book. It's my hunch or wager that something
about shame is terribly important. By denying or denigrating
it or trying to eradicate it (as in the countless self-help books
against various strains of shame), we impoverish ourselves and
our attempts to understand human life.

That's a big claim, and I will not be laying out a general
theory to back it up. To be honest, I had thought that shame

was a fairly manageable topic for a small book. I now see that it is huge and engages many different disciplines and many aspects of human life. Many have written that it is somehow shameful to speak of shame. I cannot possibly do justice to shame. One thing I have learned is that shame enforces modesty, just as it tugs at the writer's desire to explore "the big questions." This book should be seen as just that: an attempt to follow the different lines that lie coiled within shame. In small ways, I hope to use shame to nudge readers to question their assumptions about the workings of our bodies and their relations to thinking; about the nature of emotions in daily life and in academic reflection; and about ways of writing and relating.

Is shame cultural or physiological, or does it—and this is my bet—demand a way of rethinking such oppositions? Does shame disconcert us because we feel it simultaneously in our bodies, at the core of our selves, and in our social relations? These are big questions that are hard to nail down or even to approach head-on. I feel as if I'm tracking shame—hunting down past and present evidence of its various forms, following up some leads and discarding others that have attested to shame's presence. I am stalking shame in its different manifestations and in terms of how it has been described; I am following shame because of where it might lead. I am consumed with why: Why has shame been discounted? Why does shame seem so innate when it is felt, seemingly, only in the actual or remembered presence of others? Why are we so afraid of shame?

Tackling shame brings to mind the image of Sisyphus and his rock—up he pushes it, only for gravity to exert its will. Human against rock, and it seems that the rock or at least the forces of nature will always win. However, against a tragic reading of an absurdly large project that must fail, Albert Camus famously argued that the efforts of man, while absurd, are also twinned with happiness. In Camus's reading, Sisyphus is an absurd hero because of his passions and struggles: "The struggle itself towards the heights is enough to fill a man's

heart. One must imagine Sisyphus happy." Camus explicitly
links his own struggles as a writer, "to live and to create . . .
to reside in the reflection, alternately cold and impassioned,"
to the struggles of Sisyphus consigned to eternity in his task.
In other words, when we take on the absurd task of trying
to describe that which even after multiple attempts evades
us, we must nonetheless remain faithful to that exigency:
"Describing—that is the last ambition of absurd thought."
We acknowledge the impossible nature of our task and remain
honest to the impetus of our attempts to understand the seemingly infinite variety of human behavior. We describe and
describe again, write and rewrite, get lost and find ourselves
in unusual places. As Camus puts it, science itself looks on to
"the ever virgin landscape of phenomena." And he urges all
writers—artistic, scientific, philosophical, sociological—to do
the same, promising that "the heart learns thus that the emotion delighting us when we see the world's aspects comes to us
not from its depth but from their diversity."[4] Describing shame
plunges us into that diversity.

WHAT'S WRONG WITH FEELING?
Camus's words reveal great human truths with wonderful
intimacy. However, they need to be relocated in our times
and in relation to present concerns. The passions with which
Camus contended were of a unique order: the experiences of
the two world wars were still very much present; the process of
untangling French imperialism in North Africa was brutally
acute. By contrast the passions that mark our times are harder
to categorize. Fear, boredom, terror, anger, shame—it's hard
to hear what people are feeling. This book does not pretend
to chart public feeling, but does take seriously the fact that
feelings are important. While they certainly can be channeled,
they do not easily map onto any one political agenda.

In Australia, recently there have been two most remarkable
eruptions of feeling, which did not neatly conform to any one

political agenda. The first followed the release of a report in 1997 by the Human Rights Commission about the removal of Aboriginal children from their families. Known generally as the scandal of the Stolen Generations, the events described in the report were met with widespread and very public expressions of shame. Not long afterward, while those feelings still simmered, the celebration of the 2000 Olympics in Sydney provided another distilled moment of public feeling. It came to a head when the Aboriginal athlete Cathy Freeman won a gold medal for the 400-meter race. As she ran her lap of honor wrapped in both the Australian and Aboriginal flags, the nation cried with joy. In the prelude to the games, national shame was showcased as television crews from all over the world captured the truly awful living conditions of Australian Aboriginals. But once the games were under way, joy and pride, mingled with shame, interest and excitement, and different thoughts and futures were openly aired.[5]

It's easy to make too much of these momentary public outbursts; it is also easy to be dismissive of what they might represent. In one instance, people talked openly of their shame; in the other, of their joy and pride. In chapter 3, I describe in some detail the expressions of shame about the Stolen Generations and the context in which they circulated. The public expression of emotion has not been taken up by critics as widely as one might have thought. Strangely enough, some of the most severe critics of public feeling have been feminists and other "progressives." At its crudest this can be summed up as "They voted for a conservative government. Who cares what middle Australia (or America) feels?"[6] Here I want to address why and how some critics flee from public feeling.

One prominent critic of public sentiment, Lauren Berlant, an American feminist well known for her work on different forms of queer identity, investigates the ways that "painful feelings" in the United States are mobilized. It is an interesting argument against what she calls "national sentimentality."

Focusing on how "scandals" in the United States produce
a general outcry (her example is about sweatshops), Berlant
argues that sentimentality "operates when the pain of intimate others burns into the conscious of classically privileged
national subjects, in such a fashion that they feel the pain of
flawed or denied citizenship as their pain." In other words,
through the media's representation of different forms of suffering, privileged citizens get a glimpse of pain and thereby gain a
certain sense of empathy, without, of course, having to endure
the conditions that produce pain. This constitutes a climate
of second-hand, or vicarious, feeling. Berlant's argument is
that feelings, and especially bad feelings, produce an illusion
of truth: "People believe that they know what they feel when
they feel it, can locate its origin, measure its effects." She sums
this up as "feeling politics," which she says "claims a hard-
wired truth, a core of common sense . . . beyond ideology,
beyond mediation, beyond contestation."[7]

It's certainly true that vicarious pain has been central to
numerous campaigns over the years—from starving children
on the back of upmarket magazines, to the spectacular politics
of Sir Bob Geldof and others. It seems that a little bit of pain
can make you feel better about yourself. Berlant is critical of
the way in which feelings have become what she calls the site
of "public pedagogy."[8]

The trade in feelings is limited in what we can learn, but
it may be part of the critic's responsibility to specify feelings.
Interestingly, in the final section of her argument Berlant
does talk about another feeling, quite different in kind from
the generalized sentimentality she has ascribed to a privileged
American public. Berlant focuses on a self-help book on preg-
nancy.[9] Berlant claims that the book "releases women from
shame about the ambivalence they feel toward the fetus and
the theft of ordinary life the fetus engenders."[10] I have some
reservations about whether shame can be unlearned, or what
it would mean to "deshame" oneself. Against attempts to do

away with shame, I want us to embrace the sometimes painful ways shame makes us reflect on who we are—individually and collectively.

A FEMINIST DISCIPLINE OF THE EMOTIONS?

What is it about feelings that causes critics to flee? I am especially interested in the ways feminists grapple with making sense of emotions, because as women we have been historically associated with the realm of feeling. As an initial exploration, I turn to an argument about emotion in feminist epistemology. To my knowledge, Alison Jaggar's article in the canonical feminist text *Gender/Body/Knowledge* was one of the first in the contemporary period to discuss what emotion might mean to feminism. Jaggar, a philosopher, proceeds from the now overused maxim that women and the emotions are associated via an alignment of "the irrational, the physical, the natural, the particular and the private" with the female.[11] More intriguingly, she cites Plato's model of emotions "as horses needing control by character." Jaggar then clearly outlines different views on the emotions: as intentional, as social constructs, as active engagements, and in terms of evaluation and observation. She then develops an argument against "the myth of dispassionate investment," characterized by positivist traditions, and argues that contra "an emotional hegemony," there may also be potential for emotional subversion.

In the main, Jaggar's description is straightforward. She sets out what she sees as a dominant positivist view that emotions get in the way of rational methods of research and argument. Against this argument for objectivity and verification, she argues that emotions are involved "at a deep level in all observation"[12]—a point with which it is hard to disagree. The thrust of her argument, however, is aimed at sketching out the difference between hegemonic emotions—those that serve dominant interests—and feminist ones.[13] To begin, she defines "mature human emotions [as] neither instinctive nor

biologically determined, although they may have developed
out of presocial, instinctive responses." Imbued with norms,
emotions become dangerous: our "emotional constitution" is
likely to be "racist, homophobic, ambitious and contemptuous
of women."[14] Whether the inclusion of ambition seems strange
or merely a product of the time in which the article was written, what hegemonic emotions do is even more worrisome:

> These conservative responses hamper and disrupt our at-
> tempts to live in or prefigure alternative social forms, but
> also, insofar as we take them to be natural responses, they
> blinker us theoretically. . . . They blind us to the possibility
> of alternative ways of living.[15]

The force of this feminist suspicion of emotion is quite
shocking. Emotions are presented as a vehicle for voicing racism, homophobia, and sexism. In an interesting turning of the
tables, this argument implicitly portrays sexist men as overly
emotional. Against these bad hegemonic feelings, Jaggar
argues for "feminist emotions." "Emotions become feminist
when they incorporate feminist perceptions and values." So
"anger becomes feminist anger, pride becomes feminist pride."
If this sounds a little wacky, it is followed by an argument
about "how the increasing sophistication of feminist theory
can contribute to the reeducation, refinement, and eventual
reconstruction of our emotional constitution."[16]

Predictably, perhaps, Jaggar finds problematic the dominant distrust of emotion as evidenced in positivist arguments
about disinterested observation. She then mounts an argument
as to why we should distrust dominant emotions: we live in
a racist society, so our emotions are bound to be racist. This
depicts emotion as a conduit for the bad feelings that have
been shaped by society. Emotions are to be distrusted because,
Tourette's-like, they will cause us to spout sentiments that are
racist, sexist, and so on. However, using feminist theory as a
therapeutic tool, we can retrain our emotions, the goal being

to replicate the emotions of the oppressed. Except for the example of "good feminist anger and pride," we're left to wonder which emotions of the oppressed she has in mind.

An article by Margaret Olivia Little in 1992, published in the feminist philosophy journal *Hypatia,* argues that emotion, properly used, allows us "to see" different aspects of social life. "In order to 'see' the moral landscape clearly, in order to discern it fully and properly, one must have certain desires and emotions."[17] Like Jaggar, she argues that "the ideal epistemic agent herself would have appropriate affect." The good feminist subject would have the "right" emotions, and she would engender "good" emotions in others.

It's a wildly utopian vision, filled with automatons perfectly programmed with the correct emotional vocabulary.[18] These two examples encapsulate enduring ideas and preconceptions about emotion. For instance, in Martha Nussbaum's recent book on the emotions, there is a clear indication that some emotions are better than others and ought to be encouraged by public policy.[19] More generally, of course we can admit that some emotions are nicer than others. However, the very vagueness with which emotion is discussed raises the question of who is to judge which emotions society should promote. Because emotions are not distinguished, distrust of them becomes pervasive. In Susan Oyama's apt phrase, there is a lot of "definitional 'lumping'" going on. Lumping allows "all sorts of behavior, feelings, intentions, and effects of actions [to be] grouped together as aggressive."[20]

In much of the work on feelings, emotion, and affect, there is a lot of lumping, for example, of "the emotions" or of "affect." This frames emotions as inevitably and already captured by political definitions. The articulation of emotions places them as either conservative, as in Jaggar's fear of racist and sexist emotions, or futile excuses in the face of real problems; for instance, Berlant's argument is squarely against "the sense that changes in feeling . . . can amount to substantial social change."21 Their accounts are based in different arguments but share a general distrust about what the public might be feeling.

All this suspicion of feelings can make one paranoid. Certainly, I have encountered unease when giving papers about my interest in shame. The responses to them may have occurred for any number of reasons, ranging from simple lack of interest to a visceral reaction against the very idea of shame. As we would all attest, sometimes it is hard to distinguish the emotional expressions of others. I do, however, clearly remember a moment when I was giving a paper on shame at a conference. The paper has long since vanished, as have the notes I took afterward on the audience's reaction and my response. I was talking about shame and anorexia, disgust and fat bodies,22 and I remember quaking as I put overheads on the projector. I'd probably given something like a hundred conference papers by that time, so the shaking was unusual. I looked at my audience. My voice caught as my gaze encountered blankness in return. All I could feel was unease, even contempt. In the question period afterward, there was an absolute absence, a void of interest and engagement. I felt undone; I felt ashamed of my display, which seemed highly emotional in the vacuum of the conference room. I went home and had a good cry and then phoned one of the women on the panel, Jennifer Biddle, whose work on shame precedes mine and has shaped my interest.23 We agreed it was a thoroughly strange session.

INTERESTING DESCRIPTIONS

In the face of an undifferentiated lumping together of emotion and affect, I want to try to clarify the difference between the two terms. A basic distinction is that emotion refers to cultural and social expression, whereas affects are of a biological and physiological nature. As will be clear, I am interested in very different descriptions of shame, from different branches of psychology (clinical, evolutionary, and theoretical), anthropology, and sociology. While hardly a Pauline conversion, my earlier suspicion of some aspects of these disciplines seems to have vanished under the weight of this new interest. Because of the context in which I trained as a graduate student, when *essentialism* was a bad word, I have tended to veer away from both psychology and psychoanalysis. In those heady years of battle during the mid- to late 1980s, which characterized the rise of cultural "theory" in North America, it sometimes seemed you were either on the side of Foucault and Deleuze or "into" Lacanian psychoanalysis. The connotation of solidarity as blind following—being on the side of Foucault compared with being sucked into psychoanalysis—hints at some of the hostility and silliness of the time. It seemed that we, my fellow students and I, became adept at vigilance. If you let one psychologizing remark through, that'd be it. You'd be called a humanist—at the time, an epithet of considerable abuse.

The passion of such boundary marking is, for me, now harder to sustain. In my reading on shame, it's hard to conclude that any one discipline has the "right" approach. Shame is "owned" very differently by different disciplines, so the question arises of what to do with the claims to truth of the different research I draw upon. Or, in another language, what are the conditions of possibility? What assumptions have to be in place for various statements to be made? In this project I'm not so concerned with such preoccupations. This is not to say that anything goes. I am interested in different descriptions, not for their underlying truth, but for what they reveal about aspects of shame.

Instead of the term *conditions of possibility,* I now tend to overuse *interest.* It is a reaction to reading: "Hmmn, isn't that interesting?" It's neither a studied expression of wonderment nor a naive deployment of ignorance. It is an attitude guided by the question: what would shame do if we were to think about it like this, or like this, or like that? That is, how does shame make us think differently? What do radically different ideas about shame do to our understanding of it? What do they do to our deeply held assumptions and prejudices? If someone says that all humans blush (as Darwin did and many others following him), what does it do to our sense of shame? What does it do to our ideas about the body? What does it do to ideas about being wired as human? Do animals blush? According to Darwin, and as any pet owner would concur, they certainly seem to express shame. As I watch my cat turn away after I've chastised him, I wonder at his feeling of shame.

All these very different ideas are interesting. But I also use *interest* in a more specific way. Interest constitutes lines of connection between people and ideas. It describes a kind of affective investment we have in others. When, for different reasons, that investment is questioned and interest is interrupted, we feel deprived. Crucially, that's when we feel shame. That little moment of disappointment—"oh, but I was interested"—is amplified into shame or a deep disappointment in ourselves. Shame marks the break in connection. We have to care about something or someone to feel ashamed when that care and connection—our interest—is not reciprocated.

I take these ideas from the psychologist Silvan Tomkins. As we'll see, Tomkins bases his theory of shame on clinical studies of what the body does when it feels. His research, conducted during the 1950s and 1960s, was largely ignored or unheard of in the humanities. However, several years ago the well-known literary critic Eve K. Sedgwick edited a collection of Tomkins's writing, with the help of Adam Frank, then a PhD student. Sedgwick and Frank describe the joy they felt when they first encountered Tomkins's work:

> We got our first taste of Silvan Tomkins when we were looking for some usable ideas on the topic of shame. In a sodden landscape of moralistic or maudlin *idées reçues* about what is, to the contrary, the most mercurial of emotions, Tomkins' formulations startle: for their sharpness and daring, their amplitude, and a descriptive levelheadedness that in the dispiriting context sounds almost surreal.[24]

As they go on to describe, Tomkins "places shame, in fact, at one end of the affect polarity *shame-interest*." It was the next clause that caught me and has held me in its sway ever since:

> suggesting that the pulsations of cathexis around shame, of all things, are what either enable or disenable so basic a function as the ability to be interested in the world.[25]

The idea is extraordinary. It is totally counterintuitive to link shame (such a debased feeling) with interest: shame "only operates after interest and enjoyment has been activated, and inhibits one or the other or both. The innate activator of shame is the incomplete reduction of interest or joy."[26] This frames shame in a different light. The pairing of shame with interest or, even more extraordinary, with joy prompts all sorts of questions. Shame illuminates our intense attachment to the world, our desire to be connected with others, and the knowledge that, as merely human, we will sometimes fail in our attempts to maintain those connections.

In Sedgwick and Frank's account, interest operates on a number of levels. Substantially, as in the above quotation, without interest there can be no shame; conversely, shame alerts us to things, people, and ideas that we didn't even realize we wanted. It highlights unknown or unappreciated investments. Viewing shame in this way must disabuse us of shame's reputation as a miserabilist condition. It is, in Sedgwick and Frank's words, anything but maudlin. This isn't to say that shame is easy. As Tomkins clearly sets out again and again, the major reason for an intellectual and political interest in shame is that "shame strikes deepest into the heart of man. . . . Shame is felt as an inner torment, a sickness of the soul."[27] It is the affect—for Tomkins, shame is innate and biological in its inception—that shows most clearly the human organism in its frailty. This portrays shame as a kind of flashing light indicating the onset of the breakdown of humanity. But shame also comes in different hues of intensity.[28]

So shame is not always white-hot; sometimes it's felt in warm pink shyness, embarrassment, or in any of the variations along the continuum of shame-humiliation. To paraphrase Tomkins's description, shame can be activated only in situations where interest and/or enjoyment are not completely reduced. If shame and interest are intimately intertwined, what constitutes interest is large. In allying interest with enjoyment, Tomkins leads us to think that interest will be agreeable. And in terms of his insistence on the physiology of the affects, we can say that interest feels good. However, it may be at a level of feeling for which we have no words. He also pairs interest and excitement, which again the body may feel in different ways: from a response of eyes wide open and pulse elevated to a more generalized feeling of expectation, overstimulation, or even irritation. At one level it may be the result of a lot of stimuli hitting parts of the brain; at another this may be translated into particular reactions or attitudes.

The breadth with which we need to understand interest is important, and I am not making the claim that shame is "good" because it is tied to a positive, as in "good," feeling. Rather, interest is positive in its sense of being opposed to a negative or substrative state: it adds rather than takes away. In line with what Foucault would call positivity, shame is always productive. In this sense, it produces effects—more shame, more interest—which may be felt at a physiological, social, or cultural level. When we feel shame it is because our interest has been interfered with but not canceled out. The body wants to continue being interested, but something happens to "incompletely reduce" that interest.

The interest in play will take many forms: the interest the body displays in proximity to another body, or face, or eyes; the excitement of desire; the intellectual interest of why; the interest registered on the skin in relation to natural beauty; and so on. These different permutations make shame both a specific and a general optic through which to engage with a number of issues.

This is exciting, but also bewildering. Is shame one feeling or many? Is it felt the same way the world over, or does it have very particular cultural meanings? I'll be arguing that shame straddles the particular and the universal. And it makes us question again the relation between what we understand by the particular and the specific, the universal and the general. The choice is not between one or the other: the trick is to bring the two levels together, for the question of what is considered specific will affect greatly how the general is constituted and vice versa. Theory is, by definition, generalizing; it abstracts from the minutiae of concrete experience. My strategy is to bring both—theory and local context—to bear on each other.[29] It doesn't always work, but it was with a jolt of recognition that I read Tomkins's description of his analytical approach:

> The key to both Science (and Psychology especially) and Art is the union of specificity and generality—and this is extremely difficult since the individual tends to backslide either in one direction or the other—becoming overly concrete or overly abstract. I know this is a major problem of my own—but I think it may be a more general one.[30]

As Sedgwick and Frank point out, with sometimes brutal clarity, current cultural theory seems uninterested and uninteresting. Everyone seems to know the answers, because the questions are so narrow. But if, say, "poststructuralism" is the answer to everything, how interesting can the questions be? What is missed in the easy rejection of anything that doesn't fit into these narrow confines? Denunciation is easier than invention. As Sedgwick and Frank put it, "The moralistic hygiene . . . is available to anyone who masters the application of two or three discrediting questions." They continue:

> How provisional, by contrast, how difficult to reconstruct and how exorbitantly specialized of use, are the tools that in

any given case would allow one to ask, What was it possible to think or do in any given moment of the past, that it no longer is?[31]

Like Tomkins, I've been a backslider between the overly concrete and the overly abstract—more often than not in the same article or book. But I'm increasingly cranky with theoretical descriptions that are so abstract as to be meaningless. For instance, the other day my young colleague Fiona Probyn and I were discussing the question of privilege. At a conference she had been called on her uncritical presumption of privilege as a white feminist. This sent her into a tailspin of angst and self-doubt. She is embarking on an ambitious and important project analyzing the silence in Australia about white fathers who sired the mixed-race children taken from their families (the issue at the heart of the Stolen Generations). Fiona interpreted the question as relating to the idea that unless she "undid" her privilege as a white woman, she would remain complicit in this history of oppression.

Never one to remain idle, Fiona wrote a paper in which she investigated the question of how to give up power and privilege. It was a well-written explanation, citing the wide literature by both black and white feminists on the subject. My response— as her cranky older colleague—was rude: "Write five hundred words on how your privilege will detract or add to your project, and why you are interested in the case of white fathers."

Even for me this outburst was a bit much. But we had a laugh about exposing "Probyn privilege," and she went off and did precisely that. Thankfully she got back on track with her project and through detail reworked the emptiness of "white privilege" into a moving and motivated account of why it's important for white feminists to engage with a history of white abuse. The general and the particular melded into a compelling account.[32]

TOMKINS'S AFFECTS

It's hard not to dwell on Tomkins's fascinating life and career. According to Irving Alexander's 1995 account, Tomkins graduated in 1930 from the University of Pennsylvania with a BA in playwriting. He then went on to do graduate work in psychology, and, after a brief stint at working for a horse-racing syndicate, he did postgraduate studies in philosophy, where he explored value theory and personality theory. He made his name by 1943 through his research in psychopathology, but it wasn't until 1951 that he presented his ideas on affect, which he thought could not be derived "from an analysis of psychopathology but rather from a general theory of human functioning."[33] His first paper on affect was published in French in 1956 in a collection edited by Jacques Lacan. This didn't have much of an impact on his American colleagues, and it wasn't until 1962 that the first two volumes of *Affect, Imagery, Consciousness* were published. Later, volume three was published a few weeks before his death in 1991, and volume four posthumously.

He was apparently a great teacher and a warm colleague who encouraged many of the now leading names in psychology, among them Paul Ekman, whose work in the emotions took up Tomkins's ideas, especially about the centrality of the face in emotion. There is a lovely photograph of Tomkins in the opening front page of *Shame and Its Sisters*. He has one of those marvelously expressive, nearly plastic faces and a gorgeous smile. Strangely enough, the dominant lines on his face mirror the result of one of Ekman's experiments on the role of the eyebrows in emotion.[34] If lines and wrinkles indicate a particular recurring and predominant type of affect, Tomkins's face reveals a habitual expression of surprise-interest, with some sadness. Reading about all the little things the body does makes one strangely attuned to the previously unnoticed. Perhaps this explains why Tomkins claimed he suffered at different times of his life from esoteric physical conditions. From reading Tomkins, I now seem to have developed a kind of hypochondria of the face—on Ekman's scale my wrinkles attest to a life of surprise-interest and fear-terror.

Affects give us wrinkles because they are often expressed on the face. They are in a way much more external than "drives." Tomkins argues that the two systems are very different, although complementary. The drives concern the basic urges necessary for the human organism, for instance, the sex drive. They are normally thought of as the biological and psychological imperative to perform a function the body needs to survive. Sedgwick and Frank characterize the drives as digital in their on/off function; for example, the sex drive ceases once orgasm has taken place, and the hunger drive ceases once we have eaten our fill. Each is discrete in its object, and usually a particular drive will not concern itself with another object. In contrast, Tomkins argues that "any affect can have any object." You can feel anger at an object that normally causes joy; you can be startled by any number of objects; you can feel shame in the strangest of circumstances. Tomkins postulates that the affect system works to amplify the drives. In the stead of the on/off function of the drives, the affects provide a wide range of differentiation—what Sedgwick and Frank call their analogical operations.

The notion that any affect can have any object and that the affect will come in different hues of intensity struck Tomkins as a stunning idea. He came upon it in Carl Weiner's pioneering work on cybernetics in the late 1940s and early 1950s. Tomkins was trying to figure out whether "one could design a truly humanoid machine."[35] As he puts it:

> I almost fell out of my chair in surprise and excitement when I suddenly realized that the panic of one who experiences the suffocation of interruption of his vital air supply has nothing to do with the anoxic drive signal per se [since gradual loss of oxygen, even when fatal, produces no panic]. A human

being could be, and often is, terrified about anything under the sun. It was a short step to see that excitement has nothing to do per se with sexuality or with hunger, and that the apparent urgency of the drive system was borrowed from its co-assembly with appropriate affects as necessary amplifiers.[36]

As I followed Tomkins in his excitement, the idea of the affects as amplification began to sink in. It makes sense, or opens a little window into a different way of thinking. How would Tomkins's theory be applied to seemingly intractable conditions such as anorexia nervosa? According to Tomkins's view, it seems ludicrous to think about anorexia in terms of the drives of either hunger or sexuality. And as I read Tomkins's passage, I had a flash of memory. Transported by shame, I was suddenly back in a room with a psychologist during the time I was hospitalized at a young age for quite severe anorexia. I think my parents were in the background. The male psychologist banged on about my sexuality—did I have boyfriends? was I abnormal? I felt utter shame.[37] It was shame upon shame: the shame of being singled out and put in a hospital ward where I stood out among the really sick; the shame at my constant failure to gain the necessary weight to get out. At the time, to lose any weight that they had force-fed upon me was a victory; however, it was tarnished by the shame of being forced back into the hospital and horribly amplified by my parents' shame, disappointment, and desperation. Shame is catching, and it must have been both painful and deeply shaming to have your daughter proudly wasting away. In that little room with the psychologist, my parents, and me, the atmosphere burned hot with shame.

I also recall thinking that the psychologist was totally loony and had it all wrong. How much more profitable would it have been had he been interested in affect theory? Had he read my shame, might he have acted differently? Tomkins's insights would have alerted the doctor that the common form of treatment, behavior modification, was not the best suited for an anorexic consumed by shame, self-loathing, and tragic pride. To my knowledge, affect theory is still not used in the therapy of anorexics. I don't know if it would cure anorexia, but it would certainly help clarify the affective complex in which the anorexic is imprisoned. It would also illuminate the dynamics of affects within her family and close circles and maybe bring some help and understanding to those who stand by helplessly as their loved one tries to kill herself slowly. In my own situation, I might say that I was shamed into recovery. After I was released from the hospital, I would spend time with my best friend's family in town. Her father was my GP, and her mother an artist whom I greatly admired. Years later when I thanked them for helping me get better, my friend's mother smiled sadly and said, "I wish I could have told your mother before she died that it was only because she had brought you up so well." I was too polite to be bad in front of them, so I started eating again. The dynamics of "being good," the fear of disappointing others, and the interplay between shame and the desire for connection, then, are not just a matter of theory.

But how do affects work? Drawing on Anthony Wilden's work on analog and digital communication,[38] Sedgwick and Frank explain the importance of understanding the affect system as analog and the drive system as digital. The two exist in a relationship, one that Wilden says "undoubtedly involves constant switching." The two important points are: unlike drives, affects do not have a predetermined object—"a human can be terrified by anything under the sun"; and affects enable a "finite and concrete multiplication . . . of different possibilities." This yields a model that encompasses the binary motivation of the drives (on/off) and the qualitatively different possibilities of the affects. If the drives operate in a "stop/start" way, the affects are more "and/and/and/and." Visually put, drives are black and white, affects are all the grays. In Sedgwick and Frank's terms, this model allows us to understand "how things differentiate: how quantitative differences turn into qualitative ones, how digital and analog representations leap-frog or interleave with one another."[39]

How things differentiate—how simply they frame one of the more pressing questions of our times. The dominant mindset has so obsessively focused on sameness and difference that we may have overlooked the point. Instead of posing sameness and difference as opposing and static blocks, we might find it refreshing to think about the varying degrees and hues of similarity and difference that constantly inform human life. This immediately applies to those areas such as gender, sexuality, and ethnicity, which seem to have become frozen in oppositions: men versus women, gays versus straights, white versus nonwhite. In some ways we all share more than we don't, although of course—and often with good cause—we tend to fixate on what separates us. It has been demonstrated that we all blush, but beyond that common element, how, where, and why we experience shame and with what effects are all highly differentiated.

Tomkins's model is situated at the intersection of the element that he calls "neural firing," which is the same for all humans (the wiring of our affects), and those aspects that differ and are constantly differentiated (the social, cultural, and individual experience of affects). The differential experience of the affects is also an important basis for understanding how we are different (culturally, socially, and individually). Tomkins identifies nine affects, which, apart from an exception, are paired in a polar continuum: disgust-contempt, shame-humiliation, fear-terror, distress-anguish, anger-rage, surprise-startlement, enjoyment-joy, interest-excitement. The strangely though descriptively named "dismell" was added later. According to Donald Nathanson, a follower of Tomkins and a practicing psychologist, "each affect has its own address in the brain."[40] Depending on the density of the neural firing, the affect appears in variation. As Tomkins puts it, "The general advantage of affective arousal to such a broad spectrum of levels is to make the individual care about quite different states of affairs *in quite different ways.*"[41]

This then raises another key point: affect amplification makes us care about things. This brings us back to my earlier discussion of interest. Our interest can be aroused by so many very different things that we need a way of being alerted to what is important. Or to put it another way, so much is going on at any one moment that we need a system to make us discretely aware. This is why Nathanson calls Tomkins's a "theory of minding," or as Andrew Strathern puts it in a different context, a theory of "the mindful body."[42] When the body minds, and the mind is bodied, this produces a

> complex interleaving of endogenous and exogenous, perceptual, proprioceptive, and interpretative—causes, effects, feedbacks, motives, long-term states such as moods and theories, along with distinct transitory physical or verbal effects.[43]

It's an amazing tableau, especially if you think about the interrelationship among these diverse entities as one of constant movement—what could be called propriocentrism—whereby each feeling contains an awareness of its relation to other feelings.[44] This is very much a description of "innate affect [as] the link between physiology and psychology."[45] The innateness also includes what Tomkins calls affect scripts or theory, whereby the human organism incorporates in an intimate way early affective scenes. Disparate bits of information become script or theory, which interact with the work of parts of the brain and the nervous system. Tomkins explains what happens when the mind is bodied; or is it that the body minds? It is, of course, both, and it changes our image of the distinctions among mind, brain, body, stimulus, memory, and thoughts.

> When any stimulus is perceived, that is, interpreted within the central assembly and simultaneously transmuted into

a conscious report, it may activate amplifying affect on an innate basis by virtue of the gradient and level of density of the neurological stimulation of the stimulus which it reported . . . [and] may also recruit from memory information about past experiences and amplify it further.[46]

But what of the shame-humiliation affect? Let's start by taking a description that Alexander gives of Tomkins's own shame theory (again, understood as an individual's bodily summation of his or her own trajectory of affective experiences).

He was clearly adored by [his mother] all of her life. That rather idyllic picture was disrupted by negative-affect-producing scenes that led to important scripts in his life. The first ones depict him as a ravenously hungry child for whom a wet nurse was needed to supplement the mother's supply of milk. The resultant affect was shame for demanding more than his due.[47]

This scene is taken directly from Tomkins's own description and self-analysis, conducted under the pseudonym "the Sculptor." He clearly highlights the interrelation of positive affects (he was adored) and negative ones (he was greedy and ashamed of his need). He recalls his childhood as "the magnification of paradise lost and which must be escaped, fought for, and recovered." This is defined as a nuclear script. And as Tomkins wrote of his own scripts: "I was able to trace their continuation and elaboration over many years."[48]

AFFECT OR EMOTION?

Tomkins describes an intricate model of affect as central to human functioning. In Marcel Mauss's term, which I discuss in the next chapter, Tomkins sought to comprehend "the total man"—the site where, for want of better categories, the biological and the social continually charge each other. Tomkins argues strongly that "the biopsychological mechanisms and the social products be integrated into a science of man and not polarized."⁴⁹ He elaborates that this science of man "must focus not only on the casual mechanisms underlying cognition, affect and action, but on the cultural *products* of man . . . language, art, science, as well as cerebrum, nervous system and genes." While he pursues with fervor exactly how affects work in the body, he is equally passionate about what affects do to the self and society. This can be heard over and again in statements such as this: "The nature of the experience of shame guarantees a perpetual sensitivity to any violation of the dignity of man."⁵⁰

Just hearing a "hard scientist" (which he was, at times) speak of human dignity gives pause to the silly splits between science and humanities. In terms of other divisions, Tomkins rarely, if ever, talks about emotions. His commitment to the language of affect ties him to a scientific tradition and also frames his understanding that affects are innate to organisms. More generally, however, there is a lot of confusion about whether shame is an affect or an emotion or both. Some speak of emotion and never mention affect, just as some speak vaguely of affect, using it as the current buzzword of cultural theory. For some, disciplinary loyalty tethers them to one term or the other. The term *emotion* tends to be used by those who insist that emotion is social and cultural in genesis. They tend not to include in their discussion the work of clinical psychologists such as Tomkins. For instance, in his overview of theories of emotion, the sociologist Jack Barbalet refers only in passing to Tomkins and is dismissive of his "aggressive" tone.⁵¹ Despite Tomkins's plea that the study of affect not become polarized, Barbalet begins his book stating that "emotion is a social thing" and requires a sociological investigation.⁵²

It could be convenient to say that emotion refers to the social expression of affect, and affect in turn is the biological and physiological experience of it. To an extent, this is an apt description. But it also seems that disciplinary pride keeps the camps separate when what is needed is a radical cross-fertilization of ideas. For example, Dylan Evans, a philosopher, blithely remarks on how computer science became interested in the emotions only in the 1990s, clearly ignoring Tomkins and his inspiration in the work of Weiner.[53] In heroic terms, Nathanson introduces a book on shame, psychoanalysis, and writing in this manner:

> Historians of the future will see our generation as that within which ongoing sober, sensible discussion of shame became possible and all areas of scholarship infused both with new courage and new language for human emotion.[54]

Well, maybe. Or maybe not if we can't figure out which thing we're talking about and refuse to engage with those who use another vocabulary. The evolutionary and theoretical psychologist Nicholas Humphrey gives insight into the complexity of such distinctions. He is inspired by Thomas Reid, who in 1785 tried to clarify the difference between what we experience inwardly and how we talk about the experience:

> Thus, *I feel a pain; I see a tree*: the first denoteth a sensation, the last a perception. The grammatical analysis of both expressions is the same. . . . In the first, the distinction between the act and the object is not real but grammatical; in the second, the distinction is not only grammatical but real.[55]

Humphrey expands on this to say that "sensory awareness is an *activity*. We do not *have* pains, we *get to be* pained."[56] It is tempting to make the analogous point about *being* affected and *having* an emotion.[57]

Using Humphrey's point, "being affected" tends to refer to a privileging of the body in some form. How that body is defined varies widely, and, as we'll see, Gilles Deleuze has made affect fashionable in a whole other set of debates. "Having emotion" implicitly privileges how emotions are inculcated in different cultural contexts. This is true of the descriptions of emotion in sociology and cultural studies, where what happens at a social and cultural level tends to be privileged. As I've mentioned, the important point is to understand what shame does to bodies and what connected bodies do to the organization of the social. The reason I start from Tomkins's ideas rather than more sociological and cultural theories is that I'm interested in further exploring the complexity of the body.

It's the perspective of the body, as truly corporeal, that will lead us into new understandings of how we inhabit society and what it means to embody the social. So many analyses that insist that emotions and bodies are cultural dead-end in empty statements about "embodiment." However, Tomkins's true interest lies in what the affects, understood as biological, do within and to the social. He continually crosses these two domains, especially in his descriptions of shame. Then there's his insistence on dignity and how shame makes it loom large: "There is no claim that man makes upon himself and upon others which matters more to him than his essential dignity."[58] The biological and the social are therefore essential to his understanding of why shame is so important. Of course, others have come to the same general conclusion about shame's importance, but their articulation of shame seems less immediate. For instance, Michael Lewis proposes a model of shame based in a behavioral framework of standards, rules, and goals (SRGs). Contravening SRGs produce shame, "indicating a failure of the self as both object and subject."[59] In another realm, the philosopher Bernard Williams suggests that shame involves an internalization of an idealized other to which the self has failed to live up: "The sense of shame is a reaction of the subject to the consciousness of this loss."[60]

These are important ideas, but they lack the reach of Tomkins's theory. And too often if shame is analyzed from a social point of view, its genesis in the body is denied. The evacuation of the body also makes it harder to conceive of the different pairings of affects or affective clusters: shame-humiliation, shame-enjoyment, shame-interest, and so on. That shame is always connected to bodily experienced stimuli and more widely to interest is a revelation that entirely changes the picture. It feels intuitively and experientially right. As an idea it sits well in the body: "Only a scene that offers you enjoyment or engages your interest can make you blush." Affects are of the body and, as Sedgwick and Frank put it, "affects produce bodily knowledge."[61] Shame is the body's way of registering interest, even when you didn't know you were interested or were unaware of the depth of your desire for connection.

Ideas about the body become interesting again. In more than a decade's work that speaks of embodiment, what have we seen beyond the repetition of "the body," "corporeality," or "embodiment"? Tomkins provides a different kind of gestalt for theories of embodiment. Two points stand out: that affects are innate and compel us to view the human body as a baseline in all human activity, and that the bodily thing we call shame presupposes and promises interest. To take Darwin at his word: "Of all the expressions, blushing seems to be the most strictly human; yet it is common to all or nearly all the races of man whether or not any change in color is visible on their skin."[62] Blushing is the body calling out its interest.

While the point about interest may provoke interest, calling shame innate causes contestation, as witnessed in the reactions to papers I've presented. This is expressed in terms of concern about ignoring cross-cultural variations or about promoting a model of affect based in Western notions. *Essentialist* or *ethnocentric* epithets hover in the air.

But what would it mean if we were to accept that all humans blush? We accept that the gagging reflex we call disgust is an innate function to save the species from poisoning itself. Is there a difference in the two physical reactions? Does it make a great difference that the first innate reaction is associated with abstract notions we call the self and sociality, whereas the second seemingly refers only to the body's actions?

Part of the problem people may have in hearing the statement "all humans blush" is the assumption that all people blush for the same reason and that therefore blushing's significance is universal. This is to leap too quickly from a common biological occurrence to a cultural assumption of sameness. Why should innate or universal human characteristics always reduce difference? It could well be that the innate characteristics allow for a flourishing of difference. As Elizabeth Wilson argues in her plea for a reappraisal of Darwin, "There is no pre-given identity of form or function to be found anywhere in nature, [Darwin] argues; rather there is mutation, inconstancy and radical interconnectivity that produces the identities and differences we recognise as individuals and species." Wilson argues that we must attend to the "schemes and wonders of human biology . . . while bracketing the conventional theoretical expectations around them."[63]

The acknowledgment of innate affects provides a way to understand both how certain phenomena are universal to humans and also how they differentiate in their causes and expressions at an individual level and within social groups. In the next section I turn to some findings from anthropology, which seem to demonstrate that shame is universal and innate and at the same time to show that, in Darwin's words, "truly the schemes & wonders of nature are illimitable."[64] From the anthropological material it becomes clear that shame is a productive force in many societies. I take this anthropological data in the same vein as the descriptions from the other disciplines I've cited, which is to say, reading it makes me go, "Hmmn, isn't that interesting? Who would have thought that shame could be so useful?"

SHAME IN THE SAME BUT MANY PLACES

One of the most striking accounts that reevaluates the connection between universal affects and their particular causes and expressions is A. L. Epstein's argument for the anthropology of affect.[65] Epstein's field is Melanesia, and his study is both an epistemological inquiry into shame as anthropologists have described it and an attempt to clarify "the constant and the variable." It is at once a theoretically wide-ranging and pragmatic discussion about the problems of researching shame. In ways that extend Tomkins, whom he acknowledges, Epstein inquires, "What is at the heart of shame, the constant factor in all its variability?" He emphasizes the caution with which we should read different accounts of shame, continually asking about the methods behind the collection of different sets of data and what counts as evidence of shame. In psychology there are techniques such as photographic records or reports of interviews with subjects, but "what kind of material is available for the sociological and more wide-ranging account of shame?" Epstein points out that many researchers resort to "software"—novels and autobiographies. "Direct access to others' experience of shame is so difficult."[66]

In his study, Epstein draws on his own and others' ethnographic accounts of different regions within Melanesia. They include close detail about the bodily functions that accompany different accounts of shame. Epstein's argument is this:

> There are very good grounds for assuming that what is called shame represents a universal human capacity that everywhere reveals its generic core. . . . Yet, as with other human capacities, variation is no less important a part of the picture. Certain characteristics of the affective system, not least its built-in flexibilities, allow societies to "manage" shame in different ways.[67]

This is an elegant way of framing the problem posed by shame. In terms of his research material, shame emerges as a positive force. Shame is openly acknowledged and its effects are also put to use in the management of human interaction. Epstein distinguishes two types of shame in the Melanesian vernacular: *veumaiyiyi* represents "a complex emotional state of anger, shame, self-pity and resentment"; *abutu* refers to "a contest between two parties who regard each other temporarily but not permanently as enemies."[68] Epstein considers the first to be more about arrangements between individuals and the second to be primarily within the political domain of group relations. Interestingly, they are both addressed by overwhelming the other with gifts or displays the other cannot match: one exorcises "one's own shame by casting shame back at the one who shamed by forcing him to accept a gift or payment that was far in excess of what was due or where nothing was due at all." This is what he calls the motif of "giving-to-shame." Here Tomkins's tenet about the interconnection of shame and interest can be clearly heard. In the case of *abutu,* food is used to shame those who are momentarily estranged: "You shame the opposing side by giving it more and 'better' food than it is able to pay back simultaneously." While Epstein emphasizes its different modalities and argues that shame should be understood as a continuum—from blushing and shyness to mortification and suicide—he sees "a common mechanism by which the shame-response is activated." This mechanism is central to managing interpersonal relations: "Shame in this context, then, becomes a bridge between society and self."[69]

Whether used as a broad sanction within the group or a personal acknowledgment of having done something wrong, shame in this account is deeply mired in interest in the other and the group and is publicly understood as such. The giving of gifts, the showering of food on the other, attest to the desire to continue to be interested and, through shame, to be reconnected. As I mentioned, this is a fascinating corroboration of Tomkins's central point. Of course, we could say that Epstein has merely mapped practices onto Tomkins's idea, which in turn gives them quite another sense unavailable to the anthropologist. However, Epstein is also at pains to highlight the problem of translation, which he says dictates his approach: "Rather than starting out from theoretical definitions of shame, start with the vernacular terms and trace out their meanings." Epstein makes a convincing argument about the way shame works as an embodied, universal human affect and how it is always translated through culture: "How a particular society handles, elaborates or otherwise exploits the human capacity for shame links that local variant to a wider complex of ideas, attitudes and values acknowledged within the group."[70] This shows us how individuals deal with shame, and it provides an anthropological understanding of shame's role in the ethos of different societies. Shame gets combined in different affective clusters for particular reasons. For instance, in New Guinea shame is paired with pride because of the value given to assertiveness.

In Andrew Strathern's account of the Mount Hagen people in the western highlands of Papua New Guinea, shame seems linked with fear. The term used for shame is *pipil,* which can be described as big or small. Of a case of big *pipil,* such as that resulting from being seen having sex in public or, worse, having incestuous sex, an informant tells Strathern: "Yes, that is when a really big shame comes out completely. This is a kind of shame which is inside and it comes out. The shame cannot be got rid of, so they might hang themselves."[71] Shame for the Hageners is expressed in the Melpa language as "shame on the skin," which, in Strathern's words, is "a conjunction of physiological and sociological appropriateness."[72] Shame has a positive role as a strategy for managing anger, directed either outward or inward.

> "Shame" does show on the skin, and the communication of it is heightened by explicit gestures such as hiding the face in one's hands; but more crucially, it is caused by others seeing one, from being found out. [Then it is said to be] "only skin deep" and for the Hageners, or Melpa, it cannot produce sickness in people.[73]

In Epstein's and Strathern's accounts, people talk of those who are not or cannot be shamed. As an informant told Strathern:

It is when people see us doing these things that we feel *pipil,* when they see our skin, and we feel *pipil* on the skin. All sensible people will feel this *pipil.* If someone does not, his relatives will tell him: "You have no shame on your skin, you are crazy."[74]

In another account, Epstein notes how the "shameless ones" are seen in Lakalai (New Britain): marked by "their total lack of human fellow-feeling *(pa dia nanure ra varmari),* they had excluded themselves from full membership of it; having cast off shame they were marked as moral pariahs."[75] In this way shame is a marker of being human, biologically and socially. In Karen Sykes's argument, it is even seen by some as a gift of humanity. Analyzing the writings of Bernard Narakobi, a Melanesian writer from Papua New Guinea, Sykes notes how *sem,* the pidgin translation of shame, is "an ethos and an ethic." Narakobi mobilizes "an egalitarian politics of the Melanesian way . . . situated in the ethos of shame." Sykes argues that as a writer and public intellectual, Narakobi "seeks to elicit *sem* from others, as a personal response of egalitarian relations."[76]

Again the positive nature of shame is clear. Shame produces ways of being and ways of understanding what those should entail. "Papua New Guineans define their egalitarian spirit by accepting the gift of shame. The gift burdens the soul to act charitably towards others whose suffering might well become one's own."[77] Among the Mandak of New Ireland "it is said that having *sem* is what distinguishes humans from animals, as if one's expression of it can attune others to their own sense of possessing it."[78] In this way, shame is once again seen as deeply human in its bodily manifestation and social expression. From Sykes's analysis, it is also clear that shame can be used as a strategy: in part to instill in the shameless a sense of their humanness; in part as an individual ethic of life. In Narakobi's use of shame, there is a clear sense of the temporality that shame implies:

The burden of shame comes from knowing that some day
he will remember how things used to be. He knows that he
will recognize that he once had the opportunity to shape that
present in which he will live as an elderly man, into the ways
it will have become.[79]

Just the number of tenses involved in this sense of
shame is fascinating. Shame here seems to compel a future
anteriority—in shame one feels viscerally the conditional
sense of "as if": a tense that highlights the implications of one's
present actions. This is a good working definition of ethics: to
be aware of what one's actions might set in motion. From the
present Narakobi sees the future when he will have recognized
that he had had the chance to intervene in human affairs.

DOING SHAME WELL

These anthropological translations of shame give a complex
sense of shame's possibilities. Of course they are translations,
fraught with problems of cross-cultural understanding. But
they do provide further grounds for the argument that there
is something terribly important in shame. They reveal that
it is human to feel shame and that the point is to do it well.
These accounts, in line with Tomkins's ideas, emphasize that
shame is an affect of proximity. It is about bodies being close
to one another and an acute sensitivity of one's sense of self.
The importance of emphasizing shame's innateness to our
bodies is that shame is charged with its own physiology, and,
as we'll see in the next chapter, it charges the social: it makes
the social natural in the deepest sense of the word. In other
words, it is felt—and widely it seems, on the skin, in the blush,
in the covering of the face—and it organizes particular social
relations. Shame makes us realize in sometimes visceral ways
what Epstein calls "the affective dimension to the transmission
of cultural values."[80]

In shame, the feeling and minding and thinking and social

body comes alive. It's in this sense that shame is positive and productive, even or especially when it feels bad. The feeling of shame teaches us about our relations to others. Shame makes us feel proximity differently, understood as the body's relation to itself, the self to its self, and comprehended within a sphere that is human and nonhuman, universal and particular, specific and general. I see the expression of shame—and the counterexpressions to shame—as productive of what William Connolly calls an alternative "ethos of engagement between constituencies."[81]

2

Shame, Bodies, Places

I'VE MOVED AROUND A LOT IN MY LIFE. It started early when the army sent my family to Germany. I was about three, and for my first posting we were sent by boat. There's a photograph of me smiling in a smart new coat. In Germany I went to a kindergarten of which I remember very little. I must have picked up some German, because I remember hearing local women muttering about us as the shameless invading English. We were in fact with the Canadian army, but I imagine those women, still hurting from the war, thought one foreign kid looked much like another. After Germany we were posted back to different parts of Canada, complete with our newly strange accents. Later my parents moved us to mid-Wales. For a while my sister and I were exotic, constantly goaded to "say something." Contrary to the experience of some army brats, my parents tried to ensure we went to local schools. We were supposed to fit in. We wanted to but couldn't. I continued moving on my own: to Vancouver when I was sixteen, then to France for a while, then around different parts of Canada until I settled in Montreal. I was determined to blend in and become Quebecoise, but I hadn't a hope: accent and coloring made me stick out like a sore thumb. I moved again, swearing (in bon Quebecois) that it was for the last time—*hostie ça fait ben mal.*

My body hates it when I move. Months before I emigrated

from Canada to Australia I went into somatic spasms. The tricks my body played to protest my decision seemed to come straight from a horror flick. My muscles became inhabited by an evil force that twisted my stomach into knots.

This is not a tale of woe or even a particularly unusual one. But the experience provides ample evidence of a strange little strain of shame: the body's sense of being out of place. It is a shame born of the desire to fit in, of an interest in being part of a place. That interest propels you toward exposure: the slip of tongue as you mangle a colloquialism, the moment when you don't get a joke or fail to recognize part of local lore. "You're not from here," I'm told quizzically. It happens in Australia, where I'm taken for a Pom; it happens in London, where I'm taken for an Australian. Compared with the difficulties of not fitting in if you are visibly not an "Anglo," it's no big deal. It is not the racist shaming by others. Rather it's a little shaming from within, fed by the desire to be unnoticed, to be at home—or to be at ease in someone else's home.

In some ways it's a shame that is bred from shyness, amplified to something else. It could be along the lines of what Aboriginal English speakers mean when they say "shame." Roughly speaking, the epithet is directed toward someone who has separated herself from the group: "shame girl." The cause for the separation is not necessarily bad behavior. Jean Harkins, a researcher specializing in "practical semantics," reports that "the Aboriginal feeling of SHAME does not necessarily imply that the experiencer has done anything wrong, or violated any external rules. It does involve a desire to avoid potential wrongdoing and bad consequences, and thus it seems to have more in common with *fear* than with *guilt*."[1] There are ample reasons that Aboriginal Australians would be fearful of shaming by white society. Many of the white fellas' good and bad intentions have resulted—and continue to result—in isolating Aboriginals, in making them stand out because they couldn't fit in with white norms.

Of course there is only a tenuous relation between what I'm describing as my out-of-place shame and the shame of those who have been violently dislocated and displaced. The shame of the cultural outsider is fed by a deep desire to fit in and an abiding interest in being able to do so—to belong where you don't belong. This interest may be satisfied more easily if you are relatively privileged and have the assurance of status, documentation, and so on. The less opposition you encounter, the greater the possibility there is for interest to flourish. But equally, the more interested you are in fitting in, the more you are likely to feel ashamed when that interest is not enough to allow you to move smoothly in another culture and space. Most experiences of shame make you want to disappear, to hide away and to cover yourself. But the disjuncture of place, self, and interest can produce a particularly visceral sensation of shame. It is felt in the rupture when bodies can't or won't fit the place—when, seemingly, there is no place to hide.

In the previous chapter I began to draw out different descriptions of shame, arguing that they tend to be differentiated according to whether shame is seen as an affect or as an emotion. Understanding shame as an emotion tends to privilege cognition. This view can sometimes disparage what the body does when feeling shame. Conversely, researchers who use affect to describe shame are more interested in or open to considerations of what happens in the body (and its components, such as the brain and the nervous system). In this chapter I pursue a more sociological explanation of shame within the body and its habitus. The term *habitus* comes from the French sociologist Pierre Bourdieu, who describes it as embodied history. An individual's habitus is the product of all her past experiences and is structured by class, gender, and ethnicity. It's an important concept that tries to explain how our individual and collective histories inform how we are in the world. The abstract idea of social class becomes incarnate, and habitus dictates what we can and cannot do.

Investigating the physiological aspect of shame, I enlist ideas developed by Bourdieu's predecessor, Marcel Mauss. I want to reanimate a sociological comprehension of how we feel shame, so that we may more broadly envision using the effects of shame productively. While the theories I draw on in this chapter are more sociologically based, I don't want to lose the insights developed in the previous chapter about the physiological level of shame. Here I explore how the physiological experience of shame intersects with the physicality of place. The color, the place, the history of bodies all come alive in shame.

Moving into the realm of sociological descriptions of how bodies feel requires different strategies. Sociologically speaking, it is hard to find ways of describing the body's movement, how the body expresses feeling, its affects, and how the body changes in proximity to other bodies or in different places. Listening carefully to narratives, we can hear snatches of what it feels like to be "out of place." I'll also tell stories and at times retell those of others. Deep down, all I ever want to do is tell and listen to stories. However, this can cause problems, especially when they're seen to be a mere recounting of the personal. Shameful stories exacerbate this perception. In academic writing, the coalescing around the personal, compounded by shame's intimacy, renders telling tales highly problematic. Relating one's lived experience is taken as "confessional" or as a proclamation of some truth. To those trained in Foucault's critique of the truth-inducing techniques of modernity, to speak of what one feels can be deeply problematic. This is an oversimplification of Foucault's theory of power. It fails to take on Foucault's great challenge, which resides in the question of how we can see things differently. Within the strict confines of philosophical French traditions, Foucault experimented with different genres and styles in an effort to provide alternative visions and new spaces of freedom.

I want to move away from the idea that telling shameful stories is concerned only with the person telling them. Walter

Benjamin puts it perfectly when he points to shame's public intimacy.

> "It was as if the shame of it was to outlive him." With these
> words *The Trial* ends. Corresponding as it does to his "ele-
> mental purity of feeling," shame is Kafka's strongest gesture.
> It has a dual aspect, however. Shame is an intimate human
> reaction, but at the same time it has social pretensions.
> Shame is not only shame in the presence of others, but can
> also be shame one feels for them. Kafka's shame, then, is no
> more personal than the life and thought which govern it.[2]

There is something pure about shame as a feeling, even as it publicly twists the very sense of self. And yet, shame always plays on that doubleness. It is the most intimate of feelings; it makes our selves intimate to our selves. Equally, it is social and impersonal, or at least, as Benjamin puts it, no more personal than the life and thought that carry it. The promiscuity of shame, heightened through its telling, broadens notions of what is personal and what is social. The body is key here because it generates and carries so much meaning and in ways that academics have not really attended to. We have tended to overly privilege the body's cultural meanings and have not really tried to tell the psychosomatic body's stories.[3] It's a bit of an experiment. As Brian Massumi writes, "Experimentation activates detail."[4] Personally, I don't think stories can have too much detail, but maybe theories can. Enough prevaricating, let's get on the road.

GETTING TO ULURU

At the heart of Australia there's a big rock. It's really big and sort of red, or many shades of red. Composed of arkosic sandstone, it is, apparently, the world's biggest monolith. It is 5.8 miles in circumference, 1,132 feet high, 2.2 miles long, and 1.3 miles wide. Walking at a good pace, it takes several hours to circumnavigate. It's thought to extend downward several

miles below the surface of the earth, like an iceberg in the
desert. Still referred to by some as Ayers Rock, its Aboriginal
name, Uluru, is now commonly used. The site is significant
to many groups. It is at the heart of the beliefs of the Anangu,
the Aboriginal people who have lived in the vicinity of Uluru
for some twenty-two thousand years or more. It is also at the
heart of white Australians' imagining of the country, although
many have not visited it (it's an expensive enterprise to get to
the center of the country from the coast, where 85 percent of
the population lives). This doesn't stop foreign tourists, for
whom "Ayers Rock" is a choice destination.

The Anangu are now the legally recognized custodians of
the rock and the Katajuta National Park, which surrounds it.
Uluru-Katajuta is listed as a World Heritage cultural landscape.
This recognition testifies to "the combined works of nature
and of people, manifesting the interaction between people and
the natural environment."[5] World Heritage recognition has
been immensely important for the Anangu and for Aboriginal
people in Australia more generally. The mainly Aboriginal
Uluru-Katajuta Board of Management was also awarded the
1995 UNESCO Picasso Gold Medal for their outstanding
management and conservation practices. All this recognition
does not stop a surprising number of tourists from disrespecting
the Anangu's gentle request that people do not climb the rock.
Concerned about protecting the numerous sacred sites on and
around Uluru, the Anangu also do not like it when people fall
to their death in what is, after all, the Anangu's backyard.

For the Anangu, Uluru is the site of the energy called
Tjukurpa, a Pitjantjatjara word that encompasses their history,
religion, and law. In the words of Yami Lester, the chair of the
Board of Management, "In the past some people have laughed
and called it dreaming but that Tjukurpa is real, it's our law,
our language and family together."[6] The Tjukurpa maps the
relationships, travels, and activities of the ancestral beings who
inhabited the land. Uluru is a busy place.

In the dead of winter, we made our way to Uluru.[7] Eliot's phrase—pinched from the epic journey of the Magi—made us smile as we descended from Darwin. We were on holiday. The hot days of the tropics were behind us, and the sun would now be on our backs until we turned west at Alice Springs, 750 miles south of Darwin. The rhythm of time changed as we hit the Sturt Highway. In the back, leaning against the bags with my feet out the window, my body slowed to take in the subtly changing landscape. Nature stops and tea breaks gear-shifted the smooth flow of time and space. I wondered again and again at the marvel of a billy boiling in minutes, perched on a nest of twigs. It was all so new, in such an ancient land. The dryness was pervasive; the land yielded up a sigh when I squatted to pee. At night we slept on foamies—a luxurious version of the swag (bedroll)—which were just little rectangles under the stars.

We turned right at Alice and, after stopping in the ghost-drenched former Lutheran mission of Hermannsburg, continued on a rough track through the Finke Gorge. The riverbed was as dry as could be, with debris left high in the branches of the great river gums from the last time it flooded. The four-wheel drive clambered up and down sand dunes and rocks. Sometimes it would have been faster to walk, but I didn't want to leave the vehicle and my companions. It's easy to see how such a radically different space could feel like home: a secure human and nonhuman capsule upon which my life depended. It's harder to know why it so displaced my real home.

On the road to Uluru we found a track into the mulga and made camp far from the noise of the big tourist buses. It was *crépuscule,* or as one of my companions said in Australian, crepuscular time. He climbed a dune and came back to say that he had seen the rock. Dark had fallen, and by the light of the gas lamp I read my novel. The rock could wait.

The next day we broke camp faster than usual. We had a destination. Despite how much the image of the rock burned in my sense of Australia, I was less excited than my

companions, who had seen it many times before. Vague feelings
of discomfort lingered as I sat in the back. Maybe I wouldn't
like it, or, worse, maybe I wouldn't have the right feeling.

After the undulations of the countryside we'd traveled
previously, the land was flat. A wide-open flatness that does
the heart good. And it was red. Well, more than *red* can convey. We drove with no sign of change to the land. How could
something that big disappear or fail to appear?

Then there it was. Awe-inspiringly, mind-bogglingly
there. Wow—a useless word, but, wow. Complying with their
daughter's request, my companions played her favorite song for
the sighting of the rock: "Beds Are Burning," from Midnight
Oil's *Diesel and Dust*.[8] As we got closer, time slowed. I breathed
in an elation that seemed to be the result of a million things
resonating. Then as I breathed out, the quiverings were trans-
posed into sobs—great, big, ugly ones. Peter Garrett and the
boys sang over them. The anthem of good white Australia
dissipated out the window and into the red dust:

> The time has come to say fair's fair
> To pay the rent, to pay our share
> The time has come, a fact's a fact
> It belongs to them, let's give it back.

I cried myself out and fell into a sleepy, empty calm. In a
daze I walked around the rock, registering its magnificence. We
drove to Yulara, the Ayers Rock Resort. Our travels continued,
but I'll leave us there, filling the water tanks and picking up
supplies.

That feeling reverberated; it still does. It can't be lifted from
other experiences along the road and wasn't quite a distilla-
tion of feelings either. It was a white-hot intensity that burned
through layers of memory and perception. I have never felt
so out of place in my life or so simultaneously desired to be a
part of that place. Who knows to what extent the song's lyrics
directed my feeling. Playing the scene over and over again in

my head, I began to recall that as the tune started, it provoked a flash of memory. I had first heard it in Montreal, sitting on the hot summer asphalt. There was nothing special about that memory, but maybe the feeling was compounded with many memories of being out of place.

My small cloudburst of emotion seemed to be a moment of seemingly meaningless affect. Struck by intensity in the landscape, my body acted, forming expressions that couldn't be named. My immediate cognitive thought, when I started thinking, was, "Well, wasn't that weird?" Another thought was, "I'm not going to write about this." Of course words came, but I write about that experience in the shadow of shame about telling stories that are not really my own.[9] However, somewhere between the narcissism of incorporating stories as one's own and the paralysis of never telling any stories, I will experiment with that moment. I'll use it to see what it can do.

SHAME AND GUILT

One explanation of my response to Uluru is that I experienced an extreme form of guilt. Uluru is, after all, the symbol of Aboriginal Australia, and some might say that Midnight Oil has been the voice of white Australian guilt. In response I'd say that it didn't feel like guilt. I also think that guilt has been overrated. Guilt is, of course, more publicly acceptable than shame, and often the two may be hard to distinguish. Michael Lewis argues that blushing "could be a sign of either shyness, embarrassment, or shame or guilt."[10] Darwin's crucial insight remains: it is "the thinking about others, thinking about us . . . [that] excites a blush."[11] While both guilt and shame are excited by what others think of us, shame goes further. Shame is deeply related not only to how others think about us but also to how we think about ourselves. Guilt is triggered in response to specific acts and can be smoothed away by an act of reparation. Shame, however, demands "a global [re]evaluation of the self."[12]

Lewis makes the argument that "guilt lacks the negative intensity of shame," which leads him to say that guilt is more useful. Others, such as Martha Nussbaum, echo this sentiment.[13] It's a contention I take issue with. While guilt may involve a responding act of remediation, it also quickly paves the way to a politics of blame. Guilt, it seems to me, is fleeting. We feel guilty, so we write a check or add our names to e-mail petitions. Then we bask in the glow of the self-righteous until the next moment we are made to feel guilty.

Compared with guilt's operations, shame is a more positive force. Simply put, shame has many more shades of difference than guilt has. This is why shame can be so painful. In contrast, guilt tends to be on/off. Within a system of reparation, guilt prompts recompense and then is done. But as we've seen, shame can revisit you long after the particular moment of shaming has passed. This is why it is important to be precise about differently experienced shames. Lumped together, shame and guilt are taken as seemingly and inevitably describing a white complex, a political muddle of pride, shame, and guilt. This is especially clear when shame is denied, when it is seen as taking away from pride—for instance, when prime ministers will not say they are sorry for historical actions against minority populations. Avoiding shame can allow guilt to flourish. Guilt then becomes the default mode for living in a colonized land. Guilt, or fear of being found guilty, produces a situation where shame cannot be admitted. Guilt leads to moralistic judgments, and public debate gets polarized for or against guilt. Whole groups are sorted on one side or other of the divide. For instance, "Middle Australia" is said to be against guilt, while the "chattering classes" (intellectuals, inner city "radicals," and so on) are said to be mired in it. This produces a situation in which those who disagree with aspects of the past and present government cannot admit to any national pride, and those who disparage any admission of guilt become the flag wavers of pride. This reinforces a tendency for "progressives" to distance themselves from the nation and for the "revisionists" to control what the nation means.

Given how stultifying the accusations and appropriations of white guilt can be, it seems foolhardy to speak of white shame. But shame, left unspoken, solidifies as a layer of intensity that never seems to go away. In Tomkins's terms, shame is paired with humiliation, which is certainly one tenor of public debate. When shame is white-hot it also seems to mingle with fear and terror. Perhaps it is the fear of having to say that we are ashamed. Tomkins also mentions that fear and terror can be burned out by simple human contact. He gives the example of holding a terrified kitten until the fear passes. Graham Little, a psychotherapist, uses the image of holding in a more metaphorical sense. Little argues that our leaders should be the ones charged with holding us until our terror leaches away.[14] It's a nice idea, unfortunately at odds with the actions of most national leaders.

The idea that shame is often connected with fear is instructive. It recognizes the ways that shame and fear strike deep into our bodies. As many are beginning to argue, the past is carried somatically, that is, in the body. Katherine Young, a somatic psychologist, writes, "Bodies are passed down in families. . . . The body is the flesh of memory."[15] If somatic psychology is a recent development, the ways in which the body is marked by larger forces as well as by personal biographies have been a key point in much sociology. In an attempt to figure out where and how shame erupts, I turn now to the work of Bourdieu, who has done much to promote an analysis of how and why the social enters our bodies and selves.

THE PLACE OF EMOTION

Bourdieu's concepts were designed to speak across the great divides within the social sciences and the humanities; they responded to an intellectual environment in which the cultural could not be mentioned in the same breath as the biological;

the social, in the same breath as the economic. Crude divisions, framed in increasingly sophisticated ways, still work to separate the objective and the subjective, the inside and the outside, cognition and noncognition, and the body and the social.

In a career stretching back decades, which began with the detailed ethnographic study of several cultures (including regions of France, the world of academia, and the more "exotic" world of the Kabyle peasants), Bourdieu asked questions about how structures considered to be social and external to the body are incorporated into our ways of being in the world. He questioned how the social is embodied and how the body carries the social. He was especially concerned with how one's habitus, or embodied history, developed early in childhood, limits the ability to move across different social circles. Elaborated in the 1960s and 1970s, his concepts promised a more grounded study of distinction and difference than previously had been achieved. As he recounts in a 1985 interview, subsequently published in French with the provocative English title "Fieldwork in Philosophy," he wanted to develop a "genetic structuralism":

> The analysis of objective structures—those of different *fields*—is inseparable from the analysis of the genesis at the heart of biological individuals of mental structures which are in one instance the product of the incorporation of social structures themselves: social space and the groups which are distributed across it, are the product of historical struggles (in which agents are engaged by function of their position in social space and the mental structures through which they comprehend this space).[16]

As is clear from this quotation, Bourdieu did not exactly write for the layperson, although he did become a household name in France (but then, so too did Foucault). To translate, Bourdieu presents individuals as agents formed by and through the experiences of class, gender, and so on. What differentiates Bourdieu's ideas from others, such as Marxism, is that the body becomes living proof of all that we have experienced. He places more emphasis than Marxists would on the ways individuals, or agents, are corporeally informed by their social positions. Our bodies continually speak of their pasts in everyday actions—gestures, manners, and small ways of being and inhabiting social space. Habitus delimits how we can move and in which spaces we can move.

An example close to home is the habitus of the academic. In order for one to become an academic, it helps to have had a family background where education was valued. If early on, reading and being interested in ideas is inculcated, you will be more disposed to the (strange) idea of spending your life with abstractions. In more grounded ways, as you jump the various hoops—good grades, undergraduate to postgraduate—your body learns to focus in certain ways. It becomes used to navigating the spaces of thinking: finding its way around libraries, putting up with hours of concentrating on some arcane passage of text. The habitus tells the body how to speak and move in conferences, while lecturing classes, when talking to other academics. As the years go by, the habitus incorporates all the rules, and the body moves easily in the spaces of academic life, what Bourdieu calls "the field." The habitus is the body's second nature; it wears often arbitrary rules like a glove.

Our bodies seem to know when they are at ease in a situation, when they know the rules and expectations, and conversely they also tell us loudly when we are out of our league, fish out of water. The field, then, refers to the set of rules inscribed on all social spaces. These rules are, by and large, unstated because we have incorporated them. Our bodies know these social rules. This "genetic" knowledge is what allows us access to certain spheres and enables us to operate within them. The rules that structure a field or a social space also repel outsiders. This is precisely what happens when a body knows it does not belong within a certain space (to recall my designation of out-of-placeness): in Bourdieu's terms, there is a schism between the habitus and the field. This is where shame often erupts.

Of the great names who, in the late twentieth century, set the agenda in the humanities and social sciences, Bourdieu is a rare sociologist among the philosophers. He was, of course, a French sociologist and therefore heavily influenced by philosophy, even as he rejected much of the doxa of the time. He was blunt about his ennui with the established ideas that then continued to frame research in France—existentialism, structuralism, and Marxism. He was scathing about the tenor of some intellectual debates, especially in response to being called dogmatic by his opponents:

> I find it quite ridiculous that sociologists or historians, who are not always the best equipped to enter into philosophical discussions, today are reviving the debate of aging thinkers from the Belle Époque to save spiritual values against the menaces of science. The fact that nothing can be found to oppose a scientific construction other than a metaphysical thesis seems to me to be an obvious sign of weakness.[17]

While he was harsh about the limits of his discipline, his work has inspired sociological and anthropological attention to the practices of everyday life. In this the habitus is crucial; it is the space of incorporation—a favorite Bourdieusian term— where the force of history gets played out in our ways of positioning ourselves and being in the world. Habitus describes how and why individuals cannot move beyond the limitations inbred at an early age. Bourdieu was most interested in how social class is reproduced in everyday ways. But as a concept, habitus is less useful in generating ideas about how people are able to change.

While the body and the social come together in much of his work, Bourdieu was also rather vague about the place of emotion within the habitus: is emotion important, or is it a

side issue compared with the big questions about class and
social capital? Bourdieu's interest lay in how to account for
practical knowledge—the stuff that people gather and deploy
in their everyday lives and that constitutes for Bourdieu the
real reason that one does sociology. Hear, for instance, in the
following quotation the way the researcher has to be attuned
to the world:

> One has to situate oneself *within* "real activity" as such, that
> is in the practical relation to the world, the preoccupied, ac-
> tive presence in the world through which the world imposes
> its presence, with its urgencies, its things to be said and done,
> things made to be said, which directly govern words and
> deeds without ever unfolding as spectacle.[18]

Sifting through this densely worded passage, one catches a
glimpse of what might be called a raw sociology. The researcher has to be open, even porous, to the rules, the dispositions,
and the actions that constitute social life.

The habitus *generates* practices, frames for positioning oneself in
the world, and indeed ways of inhabiting the world. And ana-
lytically it acts as an optic into that world. These two sides come
together in his phrasing of the habitus as "a metaphor of the
world of objects, which is itself an endless circle of metaphors
that mirror each other ad infinitum." In Bourdieu's conception,
habitus allows us to understand how the objective and subjective
worlds of sociality coincide. In one of the many lovely phrases
that tend to get lost in his prose, Bourdieu states that "the
habitus—embodied history, internalized as second nature
and so forgotten as history—is the active presence of the
whole past of which it is the product."[19]
    There is, I think, something quite poignant about
Bourdieu's insistence on how our histories haunt us. Social
rules become inscribed in our dispositions: how we see
ourselves and the extent to which we are able to envision

alternative outcomes to those histories. This is for me captured by the way the habitus delivers a history that is "both original and inevitable."[20]

Poignant though this may be, Bourdieu does not wax lyrical about emotions. On one reading, he seems almost dismissive:

> Emotion . . . is a (hallucinatory) "presenting" of the impending future, which, as bodily reactions identical to those of the real situation bear witness, leads a person to live a still suspended future as already present, or even already past, and therefore necessary and inevitable—"I'm a dead man"; "I'm done for."[21]

Here, emotion projects the habitus's tendency to frame and adjust continually between the unlikely (the improbable) and the likely (the probable). This can be clearly heard in Bourdieu's description of how "agents 'cut their coats according to their cloth' and so to become the accomplices of the processes that tend to make the probable a reality."[22] In this rather dour depiction of the workings of the habitus, emotion seems to presage the inevitability that aspirations are severely tailored by reality. Either hallucinatory or fatalistic, emotion seems to be the body's way of registering its return to "the present of the presumed world, the only one it can ever know."[23] There are no flights of fancy possible here; emotion acts like the miner's canary, and hope is snuffed out.

Which emotion produces the statement "I'm done for"? At once it is the cry of fear and the realization that there's nothing left to fear but fear itself. The sense of emotion as anticipation/resignation before the worst is joined elsewhere by an aside to Freud's conception of hysteria. Hysteria, says Bourdieu, "takes expressions literally, really feeling the heart-rending or the smack in the face to which the speaker refers to metaphorically."[24] These are shocking examples. It's such a feminized tale of abuse. This is not to say that Bourdieu exclusively genders emotions as feminine, as the phrase "I'm a dead man" demonstrates.

Nonetheless, one wonders why Bourdieu has taken up this classic example of emotion that is located literally in the woman's womb—the *hustera*. The threat of being called hysterical certainly haunts women: that moment when a woman expresses emotion only to be dismissed as hysterical. Whether or not Bourdieu is imputing a sexual division of emotion, his example could not be more obviously rooted in the body. The implicit gendering of emotions in this example of hysteria becomes even more intriguing in relation to Bourdieu's discussion of how the "fundamental oppositions of the social order . . . are always sexually overdetermined." He supports this with an example about the "lowering or bending of the head or forehead as sign of confusion or timidity, and also shame and modesty." His conclusion: "male, upward movements and female, downward movements . . . the will to be on top, to overcome, versus submission." It is *"as if* the body language of sexual domination and submission had provided the fundamental principles of both the body language and the verbal language of social domination and submission."[25]

In this manner, the body's expressions—including that classic one of shame, the hanging of the head—act as a metonym for the wider structures of social domination. Blushing stands in for everything that makes me ashamed, including the informative early experiences of class and gender. The blush tells of the sum total of all that has made me.

This becomes more explicit in Bourdieu's discussion of belief and the body. "Practical belief," he argues, "is a state of the body. . . . Enacted belief [is] instilled by the childhood learning that treats the body as a living memory pad." This learning ensures that values are "made body," and it instills a "whole cosmology." Belief—what he calls "the almost miraculous encounter between the habitus and the field"—is then crucially linked to emotion's role in animating the body. Emotion and bodily gymnastics are central to this premise: "It is because agents never know completely what they are doing that what

they do has more sense than they know." It is the simple act
of "re-placing the body in an overall posture which recalls the
associated thoughts and feelings."[26] These acts of the body in
emotion then are key to the work of symbolic capital, arguably
the most valued of the forms of capital in Bourdieu's well-
known theory of distinction.[27]

> Symbolic power works partly through the control of other
> people's bodies and belief that is given by the collectively
> recognized capacity to act in various ways on deep-rooted
> linguistic and muscular patterns of behavior, either by neutral-
> izing them or reactivating them to function mimetically.[28]

From this encapsulated picture, we can say that emotion is
part of the body's knowledge. It seems to work to amplify or
reduce instilled tendencies.[29] In Bourdieu's description, emotion is not directly cognitive, although its effects may initiate
cognition:

> The body believes in what it plays at: it weeps if it mimes
> grief. It does not represent what it performs, it does not
> memorize the past, it *enacts* the past, bringing it back to life.
> What is "learned by the body" is not something that one has,
> like knowledge that can be brandished, but something that
> one is.[30]

This idea of the body as what "is" sits uneasily with
Bourdieu's argument about the "hallucinatory" role of emotion. As we are shown, emotion "'presents' an impending
future"; it causes the body to adjust to the inevitability of
the future as past. Bourdieu's phrasing of this is: "I'm a dead
man"; "I'm done for." Earlier I queried the resignation that
this expresses—a sort of sociological equivalent of "sod's law,"
where things will go bad if they can. In this description, emotion presages and confirms the finality of the habitus. In line
with this, as exemplified in the above quotation, the body can
only reenact the past. Listening carefully to the sequence of

events described, the body feels, or enacts, an emotion and then reenacts the past. The feeling body has the consequence of summoning the past, which then closes down possibilities. A spectral past ensnares the future.

This description conveys the way that life can seem to dead-end itself, through either class, or gender, or just familial instruction. "Probyn's luck," as my father would put it. While this view of life certainly has some truth, as a principle of research I have problems with it. It's a miserabilist position to take, and I think it rests on shaky conceptual ground. It ignores the body's range of affective expressions. Sometimes we weep because we are caught within both grief and joy. For Bourdieu, habitus reproduces the feeling of inevitability. However, there may also be times when emotions shake up the habitus, when the feeling body outruns the cognitive capture of the habitus.

In sum, Bourdieu's use of emotion seems to close down the possibilities for the body that his own theory authorizes. The separation of the feeling body and emotion, with the implicit role of the latter as a cognitive adjustment mechanism, suggests that the body is captured in and by the social. While Bourdieu admits the physicality of the body, he clumsily contains this within a dour and vague evocation of emotion. It's a thin way of describing what elsewhere Bourdieu so richly evokes. The exciting ideas about the body, or about agents being active within the making of their worlds, are undercut if the body that *is* just constitutes a container for what it has been. Returning to shame, we may find it compelling to think that blushing acts as a metonym. In other terms, a blush is the tip of the iceberg, the visible part of everything that makes us open to shame. An individual's habitus will determine what is experienced as shameful. However, where I depart from Bourdieu is in my wager that blushing and feeling shame set off a nearly involuntary reevaluation of one's self and one's actions. This may also compel a radical rethinking and a shift in disposition. Through feeling shame, the body inaugurates an alternative way of being in the world. Shame, as the body's reflection on itself, may reorder the composition of the habitus, which in turn may allow for quite different choices.

A SOCIOLOGY OF HUMANITY

The idea that the body continually produces new knowledges, which shake up the embodied order of things, makes habitus a more optimistic and open-ended concept than Bourdieu allows for. It certainly places more emphasis on the "mindful body" and what it can do in generating alternatives to Bourdieu's "inevitable history."

The sense that the feeling body enters into a dialogue with social structures—and that this is a mutual exchange—can be heard in Marcel Mauss's understanding of habitus. Mauss preceded Bourdieu in exploring the habitus as a resource for sociology. As we'll see, he places a quite different emphasis on the body and highlights that it is at once physiological, psychological, and social.

There are connections between Bourdieu and Mauss, although there's little acknowledgment of any debt Bourdieu might have owed to Mauss. It's apt to say that Mauss gets "straightened out" in Bourdieu's thought. Bourdieu was certainly cognizant of Mauss's place in the field of French sociology. How could he not be? Mauss was Émile Durkheim's nephew and did much to propagate Durkheim's influence in French sociology. In 1930 Mauss held the chair of sociology in the Collège de France, which Bourdieu was to occupy later. Bourdieu published three volumes of Mauss's work in his series *Le sens commun*. Marcel Fournier, Mauss's preeminent bibliographer, comments that Bourdieu seemed to find Mauss less rigid than his uncle. He adds that there are several profound links between Mauss and Bourdieu, especially in terms of their attention to the logic of practice and their understanding of sociology and the role of the sociologist as politically engaged.[31]

Mauss has been credited with first coining habitus as a sociological concept. Originally the term was used in medicine to describe the outward appearance of the face and the body in relation to the person's internal state of health or sickness.[32] Habitus is an important tenet in Mauss's striving to comprehend "l'homme total," a sociological vision of totality that, according to Wendy James, joins "the local connectedness of form and content, . . . the tangible aspect of human life . . . in relation to the body and its material experience, the techniques of work, and the rhythmic enactment of ritual and symbolic performance."[33] Nathan Schlanger describes Mauss's work as "a fieldwork of modernity."[34] In Bruno Karsenti's description, Mauss's project is nothing less than "an enquiry into the principles on which the human being is 'assembled' . . . a reorientation of the conceptualization of the social."[35]

As Mauss candidly puts it, "After having of necessity divided things up too much, sociologists must strive to reconstitute the whole."[36] Mauss's challenge includes the detailed analysis of the parts, as well as the task of figuring how to make them reconnect. In some ways, it is totality from below, one that works through example and detail. For Mauss, it is through the triple analysis of the physiological, the psychological, and the societal that one might arrive at an understanding of the total man. In this, the concrete living body, its physiology, is key: "The coordination of articulated motions by which it functions and by which it embodies and conveys meaning . . . these efficacious bodily acts [education, fashion, prestige] confirm the social nature of the *habitus*."[37]

Along with the impressive breadth of Mauss's project, there is also something very appealing about the man. In ways that must have been quite shocking at the time, and that remain refreshing, Mauss allows for human foible within his sociology of humanity. That humans habitually do things wrong or clumsily—that our actions and techniques attest to trial and error, mistakes, and sometimes plain stupidity—is not only accepted by Mauss but also often corroborated by examples from his own experience. In his exposition of body techniques, he recounts, for example, how his swimming technique was a product of a time when "swimmers thought of themselves as a kind of steamboat."[38] He depicts himself pushing through the water, spouting great streams of it. And what to say of a thinker who, on presenting his work—and his challenge—to the Société de psychologie, remarks that he was inspired in his thoughts about swimming by someone "whose initials I still know, but whose name I can no longer remember." Apparently, the person's article was excellent, but Mauss admits, "I have been too lazy to look it up."[39]

Mauss's ideas about the body and its techniques are infused with his experiences in the trenches of World War I. As Fournier's biography details, "Besides his grief at the loss of friends and colleagues, Mauss also discussed the sentiments of fear and panic he had to endure and his recognition of the physical and moral force of instinct, which animates or on the contrary discourages and isolates the individual during extreme moments."[40] While he is rather scathing about a theory of the emotions per se, Mauss isn't shy about using his own emotional experiences, which for me is a huge point in his favor. For instance, in regard to the war, he recalls, "I have also experienced fear, and how it is reinforced by panic to the point that not only the group, but also the individual will itself, even the brute instinct of self-preservation, dissolve all at once."[41] In response to psychological theories of *sthenia* and *asthenia* (courage and weakness toward life), Mauss refers again to the tripartite integration of the physiological-psychological-sociological. Within this complex, instinct is a driving force that, in some regards, exceeds our symbolic capacities. Humans might communicate with symbols, but the only reason that we have symbols and can communicate with them is that we have instincts: "The exaltations and ecstasies which create symbols are proliferations of instinct."[42] As Karsenti argues, Mauss's conception of the connection between the corporeal and the psychic is "not a causal relationship that keeps one outside the other." In relation to this body-psychic linkage, the social cannot be seen as merely that which is imposed or internalized. In the search to grasp the collective totality of our being, the social needs to be understood as "truly internal, natural in the strong sense of the word."[43]

The striking thing about Mauss's model, along with its combination of strangeness and common sense, is the way in which totality is understood through the intersection of quite distinctive elements. In other words, totality is not totalizing. Hear, for example, the number of things going on in Mauss's description of totality:

> We converge with physiology, the phenomena of bodily life, for it seems that between the social and the bodily the layer of individual consciousness is very thin: laughter, tears, funerary laments, ritual ejaculations, are physiological reactions just as much as they are obligatory or necessary or suggested or employed by collectivities to a precise end, with a view to a kind of physical and moral discharge of its expectations, which are physical and moral too.[44]

Compared with Bourdieu's equivocation about the body and emotion, Mauss goes straight to the pervasiveness of physiological convergences, highlighting the thin layer that exists between the physiological and the social. That layer is inhabited and disturbed by the feeling body—its tears, laughter, and ejaculations. Unlike in Bourdieu's view, these do not have to be contained as emotion, which as we've seen plays a crucial role in closing down the habitus. While Mauss also links the body's feelings to "a precise end," his emphasis is on the very physiology that animates the social. This gives a different picture of embodiment and of sociality; the body does not fall away before the social. The social here is charged by physicality and human physiology: the wants, needs, and desires of the body enacted by its affects. The embodied social becomes, to repeat Karsenti's phrase, "natural in the strongest sense of the word."

Mauss's comments are made in the context of arguing for collaboration between sociology and psychology. In part he is consigning to psychology the realm of the emotions at the same time as he seems to be claiming the affective body for sociology. As he puts it, "Whatever the suggestive power of the collectivity, it always leaves the individual a sanctuary, his consciousness, which is yours." Underscoring this gesture is his reserving for sociology "a few exclusively social grand facts: value, the sacred, articulated time, marginal and central spaces, techniques, etc."[45] Despite his magnanimous concession, it is clear that Mauss kept the most interesting bits for sociology. Psychology can have the emotions, but sociology gets the affective body, the key to both individual and collective feelings.

As a resource for understanding the full amplitude of shame, Mauss's model is invaluable. As it hits us physiologically, shame triggers reactions in individual psyches and at a broader social level. Its intensity cannot be bracketed, and it defies neat categorization. Mauss also gives us quite a different understanding of "the social." Beyond the bland abstraction that underpins some defensive sociological statements (as in the claims that emotion is social, not natural), the "total human"—organic, feeling, sometimes illogical, and charged with instincts and passions— is at the heart of any form of sociality.

HAS SOCIOLOGY BECOME BORING?

Unfortunately sociology has not done as much as it could with Mauss's legacy. At times it seems to run from the passionate view that Mauss had of the discipline. It also seems to have mislaid the precision of his analysis of the physiological and its convergence with the psychological and the societal. Fearful of losing its hold on the social, sociology has distanced itself from the innate, the biological, the instinctual, and the affective.

This has had important consequences. As Michèle Barrett argues, "Sociology is conspicuously inadequate. . . . Physicality, humanity, imagination, the other, fear, the limits of control; all are missing in their own terms, in their own dynamic." The discipline has lost the ability to produce insights that are "imaginative, sensual even, in that they speak to experience, which includes the senses rather than simply cognition." Her conclusion is that "sociology has become boring."[46]

These are large claims but are substantiated by much sociological research on the body and the emotions. It's a feat to make these areas boring, but by force of guarding against the intrusion of the nonsocial and the noncognitive and policing its boundaries, the body has become predictable. It is easier to use the body as an inert entity than to understand its dynamics. As Norman Denzin, a pioneer in the contemporary sociology of emotion, aptly puts it, "The body does not call out interpretations."[47] The body has its own logic, and there is no reason that it should be easy to figure out what it is telling us. Denzin is rare in his insistence that "the physiological and neurological substrate of emotions must be taken into account before psychological accounts or theories can be built." But even this acknowledgment is quickly qualified by the argument that sociological theories and accounts will be a "level above the physiological level of analysis."[48]

In terms of distancing the body's physiological and emotive unruliness, Bourdieu's habitus is repeatedly brought in by researchers to make sure we know that the social rules over the physical and the corporeal. For instance, for Terry Lovell the habitus's greatest value seems to be the way it ensures that "cultural arbitraries" win out over "the natural and the immutable."[49] For Lila Abu-Lughod and Catherine Lutz, the habitus allows for "ways of thinking about the fact that emotion is embodied without being forced to concede that it must be 'natural' and not shaped by social interaction." Abu-Lughod and Lutz follow through on ideas about body techniques and offer insights into anthropological understandings of emotion as "a discursive practice," questioning how "it serves as an operator in a contentious field of social activity." Yet their exciting discussion about emotion as "a form of social action that creates effects in the world" is ultimately contained by the need to protect emotions as "cultural products" and as discursive. Their argument is framed against the idea that "emotions are psychobiological processes that . . . retain a robust essence untouched by the social or the cultural."[50]

Clearly the confines of the disciplines and the extent to which they feel they need to protect an area of study have a profound effect on how emotion is researched. Disciplinary propriety results in a strict division, and often the body just disappears. In Rita Felski's discussion of shame and the lower middle classes, there is no mention of how bodies in their physiology might influence the experience and expression of emotion.[51] Felski writes from the discipline of literature, which may explain the odd place emotion occupies in her schema: it is cultural and discursive yet conversely interior to the self. There is no evocation of shame's deep and continuing impact on individuals as she reads shame off the surface of texts without pausing on its bodily mechanisms.

Others, such as Bev Skeggs, have mined shame in more profound ways.[52] Through long ethnographic research, Skeggs draws out the way in which respectability and shame operate within female working-class culture. This research richly evokes the constant feeling that a hard-won respectability will suddenly be torn by the body's capacities to feel ashamed and to shame. In other words, we get a real sense of why academic analyses of the schism between habitus and field are important. As concepts, they allow us to understand what happens when a body finds itself out of place. Deeply informed by the early experience of class, the women Skeggs writes about have had shame ingrained in their bodies. The shame of not having enough, of making do, of being judged by state authori-

ties, bosses, and middle-class women means that they move
uneasily outside their habitual social spaces. Bodies wear their
early class restrictions. And later in life they can still speak
of moments of shame. I look at my gnarled toes, the result of
wearing ill-fitting school shoes for too long. No matter that I
can now afford a closet of shoes, my feet bring back memories
of my mother's attempts to stretch the child allowance to new
pairs of shoes for my sister and me. And my feet still remind
me of the time she saved to buy me those red shoes I had so
coveted—and of my shame when I carelessly lost them.

From the bunions that remind me of my mother's attempts
to save us from being shamed at school to the larger ways that
shame frames individuals' habitus and curtails later possibilities of moving easily in unfamiliar fields, the body in shame
tells us so much. Or it could if we were to admit all the ways
in which it feels, experiences, and illustrates life's complexities.

But shame does more than attune us to the vast variety of
sensations that inform life; it also proposes a sensibility at once
practical, ethical, and necessary: "The appropriate reaction
to one's own shame is a type of self-transformation," as Paul
Redding summarizes Nietzsche's view.[53] From the perspective
of our bodies, madly trying to deal with immense amounts
of sensation, the most salient point about shame is that it is
always conceived of in interest. Interest is, as I've said, not
always pleasurable, but it is stimulating. When shame interrupts that stimulation, it is felt in our bodies, which in turn
reflect on the nature of the interest now reduced. The pairing
of shame and interest awakens us to our senses. "Without
positive affect, there can be no shame: only a scene that offers
you enjoyment or engages your interest can make you blush."[54]
Shame is our body's way of telling us that we are interested
and that we will continue to be despite shame's painful inter-
ruption. Shame produces a somatic temporality, where the
potential of again being interested is felt in the present pain
of rejection. It's a strange hope but a powerful one. Shame, in

these ways and more, is intimately involved in the passions of interest, including the academic ones. As Sedgwick and Frank point out, the physiological attitude characterized by shame, "the lowering of the eyelids, the lowering of the eyes, the hanging of the head . . . may also be that of reading."[55]

From the physiological to its social and psychological manifestations, shame returns us to the primacy of interest. According to Paul Gilroy, shame, understood in this light, marks "the predicament of fundamentally fragile, corporeal existence." For Gilroy, "the recurrence of pain, disease, humiliation and loss of dignity . . . can all contribute to an abstract sense of human similarity powerful enough to make solidarities based on cultural particularity appear suddenly trivial."[56] In a similar but more precise manner, shame makes us question what we are feeling, the nature of the loss of interest, and fundamentally—as many have argued—who we are, as a reevaluation of the self. As Redding puts it, this then entails a self-transformation. It would be hubris to say that this leads to a "better" person or indeed that the person who has felt shame will always reflect consciously on the mechanism that caused him to blush. Such a view would be too overarching and would again reduce the body to a knowable, limited entity. I won't go that far, but shame undoubtedly makes us feel temporarily more fragile in ourselves. And that acknowledgment of fragility may serve as a basis from which to reevaluate one's existence. In Bourdieu's terms, the rupture and loss of assurance, or cultural capital, when one is thrust into another field may begin the process of change. As I've mentioned, the viscerality of the feeling body shakes up our habitus, causing us to question at various levels its seemingly static nature.

But let's get back to that sense of out-of-placeness. In this context, shame cannot be understood beyond its sheer bodily intensity. As I've tried to indicate with the examples of Bourdieu and especially Mauss, traditions of thought within the social sciences have attended to the physiological and have seen in it a necessary component to understand the total human—the object of Mauss's sociology of humanity. At a fundamental level, one thing we all share is a biological body. Its somatic effects may be experienced differently, but the body *is*. We are human because of the physiological and the somatic. How could it be otherwise? Without that basic level, all our theories fall flat.

OF BODIES IN OTHER PLACES

And what of that example of my moment of affect left so rudely all these pages ago? Now that the memory has faded, how do I get back into that body sitting in the back of a Land Cruiser, choked up at the sight of a huge rock? Were those feelings mine? Where have they gone? The fading of emotional and affective intensity is hard to deal with. Of course, when it really hurts, you're glad that the heat lifts from the memory. Do the feelings lie quietly at the back of the mind, or are they slotted away in the body's filing system? Some theories argue that, depending on the intensity and repetition of the affect, grooves get worn into bits of the brain.[57] In some cases, severe stress interferes with the placement of mediated memories in the hippocampal localization system, the part of the brain where memories are thought to be stored and categorized. As a result, "it is likely that some mental representation of the experience is laid down by means of a system that records affective experience, but that has no capacity for symbolic processing and placement in space and time."[58]

Does this mean that some affective experiences are recorded somewhere but our brains have forgotten where? The complexity of what the body habitually does is marvelous and completely renews how we think about bodies. Shame and other affects let us know what's going on. "So much is going on in the brain that nothing gains attention unless it triggers an affect." Donald Nathanson argues that it is this "affective amplification [that] gets into the limited channel we call consciousness."[59] Children seem to be better able to pick up the various affective triggers. The world constantly enters their bodies, not yet trained with the words and previous experiences necessary to sort out what they should be feeling. The affective triggers set off a lightning process of feeling, registering, and reflecting. Think of how different emotions can pass over a child's face as quickly as clouds scud along a windy sky.

Nathanson, a biologist turned psychotherapist and a disciple of Tomkins, presents a three-part explanation of affective experience. His terms are a bit geeky, but maybe that's their appeal. At the level of "hardware," he identifies the structural wiring and data handling of the central nervous system, the skin and muscles of the face, and assorted chemicals and hormones in the body. The drives and affects are located at the level of "firmware." "Software" is what he calls the experience of life, of family background, and so on. Another way of putting this is that affect is a biological phenomenon, and emotion "represents the assemblage of any affect with our previous experience of that affect. . . . Affect is biology, while emotion is biography."[60]

Wouldn't it be something if the long debates over nature and nurture could be so winningly phrased? However, it is a formulation that is missing some crucial terms, and it also instills a gulf between emotion and culture and between affect and the body. Thankfully we're not constrained by a language of hardware and software. Some writers have the gift of conveying how their bodies move, change, and adapt to place. They describe how the physiology of the body meets the physicality of place in ways that extend scientific language and ideas. Kim Mahood, an Australian writer experimenting across the genres of memoir and novel, writes about what happens when the physiological and biographical converge. Her book *Craft for a Dry Lake* is an extended meditation on bodies that are out of place.[61] It mines the interest, desire, and knowledge of the impossibility of some bodies to be in place, or what Aboriginal Australians call being in country. Mahood delicately describes the white shame of physically being out of place in the ancient land of Australia, of a body out of place in land and history. The temptation to romanticize or to wallow in impossibility is continually displaced in favor of precise description of who is feeling and what is being felt.

> Crossing the border back into the Territory, my childhood rushes to meet me. The colours begin to intensify, the light sharpens. I begin to feel something in my bones and nerves and viscera. I would not describe it as an emotion. It is more like a chemical reaction, as if a certain light and temperature and dryness triggers a series of physical and nervous realignments. . . . My pulse is up, everything takes on a hallucinatory clarity.[62]

It's a beautiful description of the porous state I experienced while being driven through the outback. Mahood highlights very different types of interest: the colors of the land, the body's racing pulse, and the light that hits the retina. Memories from childhood push against her habitus. Later Mahood again describes her affective reaction to the land as more than an ensemble of mental images: "It is something else too, a set of visceral alignments over which the intellect has no jurisdiction." Ostensibly in honor of her father's memory, Mahood recounts a voyage back to her family's station in the Tanami Desert, a vast tract of the Northern Territory between the Simpson Desert and Western Australia. It's also an account of her affective experiences, told in the terms of her physiological realignments to the land and set against a refusal of emotion. Her father, we're told, had been deeply suspicious of emotion: "He described it as *spilling your guts* or, ironically, *expressing your innermost feelings.*" Mahood agrees with her father, although he was, she says, extreme in his "terror of exposing himself."

At one point in her travels, she apologizes to her only companion, her dog, for an overt expression of emotion.[63]

Her father had taken to drink, and in a banal way we can surmise that Mahood's emotional response to this was shame. But that would be to flatten the different affective tones she gives shame. Living with a drunk would certainly have laid the ground for an acute sensitivity to shame as well as other emotional responses. For children with such fathers, continual vigilance and observation become ingrained: "Has he had too much? Will he start shouting in front of my friends?" In her careful distinction of what feel like emotions, we hear with clarity the result of that childhood experience, a deep structure of habitus. Her writing is deeply relational, constantly making connections. She writes from one plane to another, avoiding neat distinctions, such as between biological affect and biographical emotion and between body and social. Her emotion becomes biological, because she recognizes her biography affectively written on the land. Mahood's intense description of the different planes renders categories inadequate to what is going on. The description of her journey is, in Mauss's sense, total. Humanity is glimpsed in its continual relation to land, bodies, time, and place.

Mahood writes as a white woman in relation to the land that belonged to her family and was the place of her childhood. She also writes of an Aboriginal relationship to the land. When she is invited to a women's business ceremony,[64] she finds herself automatically, or biologically, following the Aboriginal tradition of setting camp in the direction of her family's land: "that country that my father turned into a cattle station."[65] When the women's bodies turn in the direction of their country, we see the way in which humans react to the land, as plants act in accord with tropism. Our bodies react to different stimuli, like sunflowers innately turning this way and that. The relations among affects seemingly multiply indefinitely. As a child Mahood was given a skin name by the local

Aboriginal women on the station, "a formality which places [whites] in a category of relationships and behaviour." She now acknowledges the ambivalence: "It's as if I have come by a secret password by dishonest means and have hoarded it against the moment when it might open a magic door."[66]

To map all the relationships among the affects Mahood describes would take a long time. But is she ashamed? Not in the usual sense, and she pushes back the obvious emotional expression of white shame that she associates with urban romanticism about Aboriginal culture. When she speaks of her relation to Aboriginality, "her unearned title," as creating a frisson in urban society, it's hard to tell if the shame is on her or on her urban friends. Her description of Aboriginal Australia's relationship to the land draws out "a harsh sexuality" that both quashes white myths and places her, as a white woman, on the sidelines. She rejects those myths of comfort and estranges herself:

> The primordial landscape is scattered with the evidence of ancestral acts of rape, copulation, dismembering. It is about a physical encounter with the land itself, a wounding, a letting of blood, a taking of the country into oneself, of taking oneself into the country.[67]

In contrast to this unfathomably multifaceted relationship, the non-Indigenous seem to flounder. "Whites who live here struggle to articulate an attachment over which they have no control. They leave and return, resentfully, full of anger and indigestible griefs." These white experiences are "scratches on the land" that cannot be understood without an appreciation of the "price the homage to this country extracts." "Acceptance" is possible, "predicated on limited ambition: a moment by moment focus on the job to be done, the life to be lived." Life on this land seems unendurable, just as it seems amazing that whites keep at it, rearing livestock in ridiculous conditions. Mahood wants us to acknowledge that enduring the impossibility of being in this place is predicated on "a narrow and deeply grounded wisdom."[68]

Mahood's account could be understood as confirmation of Bourdieu's argument about the finality of the habitus. But that ignores the marked difference of her habitus from her father's; somewhere, somehow, her inherited habitus has been changed. Emotion and affect have shaken it up, reconfigured it, and allowed for other dispositions and understandings. Taking the effects of this deep into her writing shows that a white woman can be truly open and porous to the land, to its Aboriginality. It results in a type of acute shame-driven reflexivity that cannot be collapsed into white guilt. There is, in fact, no guilt to be found in her landscape. Mahood's affective account is predicated on interest—the type of interest that's hard to come by unless it's deep within your habitus. In her description of her father and those who stayed on as managers of now Aboriginal-owned land, there is a sense of the affective complex of anger-rage, terror-fear, and shame-humiliation. The clinical description of anger-rage—the frown, clenched jaw, red face—uncannily captures the mythic image of the tough laconic white Australian male on the land. To return continually to live a life circumscribed by "limited ambition" is to be placed within the ambit of shame: it signals, in Bourdieu's phrase, that awful feeling: "I'm a dead man." We hear again the finality that the habitus seems to guarantee. But in a more telling way, Mahood also depicts how bodies continually try to escape that finality. They act out and alongside the sentencing of "I'm done for." Simply put, they change. The physiological charge of feelings brings about new dispositions. In Mahood's account at least, they allow for alternative ways of reflecting and living.

As a cipher for a larger history, Mahood's physiological reactions again and again speak of interest and interest foiled. This cannot be understood outside her habitus, in which the physiological is the psychological and the social. The body *is*. And the body is its reactions to the dryness, the light, and history, which are enfolded fully within that particular habitus. White-hot shame is in the habitus: the body expresses such interest and then registers that the interest cannot be fully followed through. This is not, however, a romanticization of shame that can be readily incorporated into already constituted political projects, nor is it a condemnation of a generalized white history. It's harder than that. It's not a shame that can be relieved by apology.

Neither heroic nor scandalous, this white shame is deeply interested and interesting. It is not purely social and cultural (which would make it easier to eradicate), nor can it be written into some general account of a white psychology. While the physical and visceral acting of affect disturbs such pigeon-holing, it recalls strongly Mauss's assemblage—the physiological-psychological-sociological intersection. Writing that tries to comprehend this totality begins to shed light on the delicacy of white shame. If, as the affect theorists put it, we're born with a basic palette of affects, how, where, and when they move us also need to be understood in terms of different shades. If the social is natural, physical, and physiological, we need to make our descriptive language as muted as the colors of the land.

WHITE ON WHITE

And again, what of my own little example? That I keep avoiding it already speaks of shame. But the exaltation before and in the sight of Uluru can also be described as interest-excitement and enjoyment-joy. There may also have been some of the neutral affect Tomkins calls surprise-startle. The eyebrows up, eyes wide open and blinking, smiling and looking and listening; I couldn't quite believe I was there. And then the near simultaneous movement to sobbing, head down, fingers covering my face. Well, yes, these are the classic facial displays of shame. At this level, I felt the heat of shame; it ripped into me physiologically and was beyond my cognitive control.

But equally at that moment, in that tensing together of sensation, there was a splitting of shame. As Massumi has argued, the difference between emotion and affect can be described as a bifurcation in response, where "language functions differentially to intensity."[69] How can we listen and speak shame? How many stories and descriptions of shame circulate? In such a storied place as Uluru, I became aware of my shame, which referred itself back to more shame. The fact that Midnight Oil was playing cannot be forgotten. Their words cannot be ignored. "How can we sleep while our beds are burning? . . . The time has come to say fair's fair." But as I was paralyzed with shame, what words was I left with?

Some sorts of shame are easier to narrate, and the abundance of certain shame narratives can erode the potential to feel shame's effects. What we might call cognitive shame tends to override that other little shame that whispers in the habitus: the body calling out its hopes and discomfort because it feels out of place. This shame is the body saying that it cannot fit in, although it desperately wants to. One of the important thoughts to take from Bourdieu's notion of the habitus or from Mauss's description of the total human is that our bodies and their biographies may be more complicated than we've given them credit for. Conceptually, they challenge any neat divisions of biological affect and biographical emotion, of the social and the physiological. Our bodies and histories are constituted by so much more than we usually allow for.

A truly embodied attachment to the world is impossible without the force of interest I've tried to draw out here. That interest, made unavoidable in our shame, speaks of the intricacy with which our bodies operate in the world. In shame, our habitus becomes reordered, shaken up, it admits other possibilities and in turn allows for more interest to be registered. As in Mahood's example, it's crucial that different stories be told and in different ways. It's not that the effects of shame can be harnessed by stories; it's that shame demands that we tell other stories.

Not all uses of shame's effects are good. Why should they be? Shame is a product of human bodies and a fact of life, but then so too is love, which sometimes leads people to do strange and even cruel things. Like love, shame illuminates ordinary and extraordinary ways of being in the world. What we experience in our bodies gets translated into all sorts of behaviors. It is undeniable that shame can be channeled into a politics that seeks to wield power over others. But before I turn to that critique in the next chapter, I want to insist that shame, even when its effects are negative or destructive, still allows for another way of thinking ethics and politics.

3

The Shamer and the Shamed

I'VE BEEN SHAMED BY FEMINISM—what feminist hasn't?
Sometimes it's a theory, sometimes it's a speaker who uses
feminist ideas to shame others. One such occurrence happened
many years ago when I was a graduate student. A big name
came to town, an American who specialized in the reclaiming
of supposedly misogynist words. Her talk was a big event, and
she packed a very large university auditorium. We had an hour
of denunciations of men (not surprising) and also of women
she liked to call "painted fembots." That was pretty normal,
especially in those days. But what was strange was her seemingly high regard for ancient Greeks.

I was confused by this combination of topics: bad men,
women in makeup, and good dead white male philosophers.
I was also a bit hot in the room full of excited and sweaty
women. I was probably wearing lipstick—a lone fembot in the
crowd. With the foolhardiness of youth, I got up to ask a question. I had to go down the stairs to the stand-up mike in the
middle of the auditorium. I don't recall the exact wording of my
question, nor do I even remember what exactly had got me so
het up. I came out with something about why she felt the need
to use the Greeks as a bedrock of truth in her feminist theory.

"What?" she hollered.

"Um, what is it about the Greeks . . . ?" I spluttered.

She roared, "I don't understand the question." And then

she followed with a line that I have not forgotten. "What is it about these frigid women?" she asked her crowd. The crowd went wild, calling out her name and hissing at me. Unable to avoid them, I got on my hands and knees and crawled out of the room.

As a moment of shaming, it stands out. It's nothing new that feminism makes people impassioned. The potential for shame is all the greater because feminism has put forward ideals that often inspire the best in people and of which it is also easy to fall short. Equally, feminism is a complicated field, to use Bourdieu's term. It is underwritten by a plethora of rules and unstated knowledges. It's easy to trip over one's principles and easier still to trip over someone else's. Ideals also can be used as rods against others: "Shame on you."

In this chapter, I consider feminism's relationship to shame. While I focus on feminism, the critique could equally be leveled at any number of political groupings—left, right, and in between. Moral reproach is not limited to so-called progressive movements. It flourishes within groups that come together around a perceived instance of injury, and historically these have been groups of minorities: women, people of color, gays and lesbians, and so on. However, increasingly it seems the injured appear in any number of guises, for example, working-class white men who feel disenfranchised by economic and industrial changes or white men in general who perceive that their worth is debased by the rise of successful women, blacks, gays, and so on.

One could tentatively distinguish between a politics resulting from feeling shame and a politics that actively seeks to cause shame in those seen as their enemy.[1] It's a tricky distinction, because often groups spring up around sites of experienced shame, which then coalesce into fields where those assumptions and rules are used to shame others. In a culture organized around increasingly complex questions of who is hurt and who is to blame and who feels resentment against whom, shame is bound to flourish. Wendy Brown's work has been notable for critiquing current uses of a "rights discourse."[2] While the civil rights movement was a pivotal moment in history, Brown argues that appealing to the state to remedy the effects of oppression is a limited strategy.

Drawing on Nietzsche's formulation of *ressentiment,* whereby the dominated use their "injury" to claim reparation, Brown questions whether we can "learn to contest domination with the strength of an alternative vision of collective life, rather than through moral reproach?"[3] Against the dynamics of guilt that underpin moral reproach, shame may provide us with a more positive ethos. Drawing on the deeply embodied experience of shame compels a different approach to envisioning social life: it highlights the connections and proximities of individuals to one another as the basis on which political action ultimately rests. In seeking a constructive use of shame, we need first to contest certain ways that shame has been put to work within progressive movements such as feminism.

GENDERED SHAME

According to Benjamin's analysis of shame, it is "an intimate human reaction, but at the same time it has social pretensions. . . . Shame, then, is no more personal than the life and thought which govern it."[4] In these terms, shame is intimately social, and it compels a revision of theories and practices in which the emotional would hive off from the social. As I've indicated, there is a gulf between those who privilege the cognitive and those who are interested in the noncognitive. On the side of scientific analyses of affect, descriptions of the actions of our bodies are more precise and varied than tends to be the case in the humanities. There is also less concern with depicting feeling as anything other than a physiological action.

Hear, for example, the way in which Robert Zajonc, an experimental psychologist, expresses what bodies do:

> In contrast to cold cognition, affective responses are effortless, inescapable, irrevocable, holistic, more difficult to verbalize, yet easy to communicate and understand.[5]

Zajonc's confidence in the premise that affect just *is* is refreshing. So what, he seems to say, if we can't put a name to it; we know it's there. As a psychologist working in affect and neuroscience, he is apparently well known for making provocative statements. And given how he straddles the hard sciences and psychology (a discipline itself caught between hard and soft), he probably provokes different groups of people. His claim that "affect is basic"—that is, primordial and primary—has certainly challenged cognitive psychologists. For instance, Stanley Rachman, a researcher in therapeutic practice, takes to heart Zajonc's argument that affect exists outside cognition. Rachman concedes that clinical psychotherapy is "usually unsuccessful [in its] search for cognitive explanations of our many affective responses." He summarizes the challenge of Zajonc's findings: "Affect is pre-cognitive; affect and cognition do not operate in the same system." For clinical psychotherapy, the point of intervention shifts radically from behavior modification to "affect modification." It's an interesting idea: instead of managing the behavior caused by different affects, one would focus on the source. The point is to get "direct access to the affective system."[6]

Rachman admits that drugs already offer access to the affective system and bypass the cognitive, but he challenges his own discipline to develop nonpharmaceutical methods of access. One of the problems he doesn't mention is that affect may not be in one definable location. It may be all over the place. Even if we agree with the idea that "affect is basic" (which I do), it may be basic to all sorts of arrangements beyond the ken of one discipline: as basic to the human organism as it is to human organizations. As we saw, for Mauss, it is the total human as the intersection of distinct elements that is important. His insistence on an assemblage of the physiological, the psychological, and the social also highlights the necessity of accessing the affects in more than one place; we may have to work at three levels all at once. The question also has to be posed at a level of totality—at the level of what affect *does*, rather than simply what it *is*. What are the politics of shame? What are the political effects of shame? How could a full or total account of its affective, physical, and social cognitive force change ideas about how to intervene in the public sphere?[7]

In other words, we need to think through shame's passage from the physiological level to the sphere in which it becomes political. As I've argued, shame is a powerful instance of embodiment, but it is also called into being by, and then inflects, historical and political circumstance. Governments around the world now apologize or express shame to those who were the objects and victims of past practices. Shame gets named and positioned within concrete political and social spheres. The questions remain: What is the point of shame? What can it do and not do?

These questions speak of a normative project. I will discuss explicitly normative models of shame; however, my intention is more evaluative and exploratory. I want to draw out the wide-ranging effects generated by political uses of shame. I'll say up front that I think certain ways of harnessing the effects of shame may be misguided. But it's also a fact of social and political life that affect gets channeled into different emotive political movements. Shame is felt at different levels in individual bodies and in the body politic. At the personal and individual level, it may be the wellspring for all sorts of actions. In the political arena, it becomes a football or even a grenade lobbed at an opposing camp.

To give some color to these statements, I turn to two examples. The first is from the Web site www.backlash.com. This seems to be a space where disgruntled men can actively advance a backlash movement against what they see as the excesses of feminism. Accordingly, it is filled with affect and emotion. Wade Balder, in "The Me Gender" section of the site, states the following:

> While most of us shame to some degree, my guess is that women use it more than men. . . . Men have used their larger size to intimidate and control people. Women have had to resort to more subtle devices, such as shame.
>
> . . . Women will probably continue to shame men. . . . To a large degree feminism has shamed men into silence in the political sphere. . . . Shame, as well as chivalry and paternalism, have allowed feminism to get away with murder.[8]

The second example comes from a television documentary and the accompanying Web material. "Battle of the Sexes" was aired in Australia on *Catalyst,* the ABC's popular science program. "The program starts with a bang—we explore how men and women approach sex . . . emotionally, bio-mechanically and practically." From the program's transcript, here's how the research on emotional differences is presented:

> NARRATION: Raquel and Ruben Gur are neuroscientists. They are interested in how men and women USE their brains to perform a range of activities. They also happen to be married to each other, so like most couples they have a few leads.
> They wanted to see which parts of the brain are active when men and women think about emotions. The volunteers are shown photographs of faces which depict various moods. They are then asked questions about the emotions expressed while their brains are scanned. The initial findings—that women are better at recognizing emotions than men.
> RUBEN GUR: A woman is able to recognize the emotion on a

face even before she would recognize that it's a face, rather than something else. A man first has to make sure that it's a face and then starts figuring out what the emotion is.[9]

There is a nifty diagram of the female brain divided into parts, which are labeled as dedicated to jealousy, need for commitment, irrational thoughts, phone skills, shopping, and a fairly large "chocolate center." The program goes on to describe the presumably more serious research findings that women's brains have more neural connections between the two hemispheres.

> To express emotions both hemispheres are needed simultaneously. Emotional thought starts in the limbic system and is processed on the right hand side of the brain, while speech is in the left. The poorer information flow between the hemispheres in the male brain means that a man must use more of his brain to interpret emotions. So it really is biologically harder for a man to express emotions—whereas women are better wired to convert feelings into words.

By coincidence I came across these two examples on the same day. The examples seem to speak to each other, albeit in strange ways and across a gulf. They both assume that shame and affect are gendered, either at the level of men's and women's brains or in terms of how shame is deployed socially. If women are better equipped socially or neurologically at shaming, what is the connection between feminism and shame? How can we respond to those who argue that women are politically shaming men into silence?

WHAT A WOMAN FEELS

That women have been associated with the emotions is so prevalent a notion in our culture that it can go unqualified. This "common sense" underpins countless treatises that posit women as mired in the body's feeling and place men as masters of reason. It doesn't leave women a lot of room to maneuver. We can celebrate women's inherent aptitude for emotional engagement. But this has political implications. In Balder's view, biologically women have evolved a greater emotional dexterity in order to compensate for men's superior physical strength. In this framing of women's "natural" inferiority, the capacity to shame men is seen as a weapon. Of course, this also plays into a negative view of women as emotional, irrational, and vindictive.

The anthropologist Catherine Lutz has studied women and emotion cross-culturally and in American discourses. From interviews with women, she identifies a prevalent belief that women have a problem controlling their feelings. She also reports that women are commonly seen as better able to read facial emotions than men because of a "history of being primary caretakers of infants." Her concern, however, is more about how emotions have come to be understood culturally and in dominant social scientific discourse. She posits a theory as to why society associates emotions with women. "In all societies, body disorders—which emotion is considered to be in this society—become crucial indicators of problems with social control and, as such, are more likely to occur or emerge in a discourse concerning social subordinates."[10]

Ullalina Lehtinen, a Swedish philosopher, takes a different tack, asking "how to understand *what* a woman *knows* when she *feels* shame (or recognizes another woman's shame), and *how*, by what means . . . she knows what she knows or claims to know."[11] It's an interesting question: does shame feel different to women? Lehtinen discusses the reactions of an audience to a well-known and still-shocking photograph of a woman in postliberation France. Robert Capra's photo of a woman with the shaved head of a collaborator accompanied by her child seems to embody the shame of the woman. The historical context of Nazi collaboration is, of course, murky, as Alain Resnais's complexly disturbing film *Hiroshima mon amour* so clearly demonstrates.[12] In the portrayals of women collaborators during the war, is the shame on the woman, or is she a vehicle for a larger societal shame?

Lehtinen reports that the men and women in the audience reacted differently to the photo. The women tended to empathize immediately with the degradation of the woman collaborator, whereas the men wondered, "How do you know that the woman did not instead feel strengthened by her experience, did not end up feeling *morally superior* to her perpetrators?"[13] Lehtinen makes the argument that women feel an inner shame and that men feel it as outer. In other words, men may feel shame in a less penetrating way.

This connects in interesting ways with the Gur research I discussed earlier, about how men have difficulty locating and communicating their understanding of emotion. Lehtinen extends her point to argue that there are gender-specific ways of understanding and knowing the significance of shame. Not surprisingly, she departs from the brain research in her argument about the source of gendered emotional experience. Shame, for Lehtinen, is located not in how women are wired but in the cultural phenomenon of "women's enduring, historically diverse, and multidimensional experiences of subordination." Citing Sandra Bartky, Lehtinen argues that for the socially subordinate, "shame is not so much a particular feeling or emotion . . . as a pervasive affective attunement to the social environment."[14]

Both Lutz and Lehtinen raise interesting points that concur with analyses of working-class women and their experience of shame and anger.[15] In this sense, shame might be a type of feedback loop that continually connects the individual and her environment. Both from anecdotal experience and from a wealth of studies, it's clear that those who have been the object of shaming early on have a greater capacity to reexperience the feeling. In Tomkins's work, early experiences—and he places them as early as the neonatal period—ensure that we all have "scripts." These scripts constitute the "individual's rule for predicting, interpreting, responding to, and controlling" primal affective scenes.[16] Although, as I discussed previously, Tomkins's work is based in the identification of some nine innate affects, he is also deeply concerned with how our affects interact and are amplified in certain social situations. His notion of the script also foregrounds that such scripts are partial and incomplete.

Affective scripts are the ways and patterns of how life's material will be composed. In this we can hear another way of describing what was described in the previous chapter as the habitus. Our early experiences, framed by class, race, and gender, are reproduced in how we understand possibility and limitation. Events in the individual's life will be "variously combinable, recombinable or decomposable" according to the individual's script. Tomkins cites the example of a man who having suffered humiliation all his life suddenly meets with praise. The question is: how will the man integrate praise into a lifetime of experienced humiliation, which has in part been shaped by his negative script? Tomkins's answer is that he will tend to repeat the negative scripts and not understand praise. While it is possible to develop positive scripts, which Tomkins calls antitoxic and remedial, the weight of experience is played out in the nuclear script. These "appear to the individual to have robbed him of what might otherwise have been a possibly better life."[17]

These ideas have something of the clarity of common sense. Somewhere between the physiological firing of affects and the social encapsulation of what they mean, we follow the body's scripts. If individual women have experienced early in their lives primal scenes of shame and humiliation, seeing other women shamed will tend to reactivate the feeling. It's a somewhat despairing picture, not unlike Bourdieu's dour depiction of the habitus. Against these static descriptions of the structure of experience, Sedgwick and Frank's point is important to recall: "The pulsations of cathexis around shame, of all things, are what either enable or disable so basic a function as the ability to be interested in the world."[18] This breaks with the mimetic structure whereby shame is experienced as only a replaying of early experiences. As I've argued, shame needs interest in order to come into being. While it interrupts lines of interest and connection, the reason we feel shame is that we want that interest to continue.

This is not to say there aren't compelling reasons to argue for the possibility of shame-prone groups of individuals. On this point, Lehtinen argues for the distinction between "the aristocrat's shame" and "the underdog's shame": "What might only slightly embarrass a privileged person might evoke shame in the socially subordinate."[19] This happens because those who have not been shamed by their gender, class, or race have "the privilege to either internalize or defy" the prompt to shame. Conversely, Lehtinen argues that for women there is seemingly no possibility of defying the shame: "Being a woman was not considered a contingent, abstractable fact."[20] Seeing a woman shamed, "you are ashamed that you are ashamed."[21] Rather than drawing a purely causal connection—I am a woman; therefore, I feel another woman's shame—we might find it more intriguing to think about how women tend to be brought up around women, in women's spaces, such as kitchens. In this atmosphere, talk is encouraged, and empathy ingrained. Lines of interest and connection are forged from early on. Common facts of women's lives (menstruation and so on) are framed as shameful and may make some forms of shame more contagious among women.

It is undeniable that repeated exposure to scenes of shame reactivates and feeds the individual's capacity to experience shame. It's equally undeniable that a collective history of being shamed will affect the scripted responses to shame of individuals within the shamed group. The public circulation of specific scripts about shame makes it easier for individuals to catch shame. Popular culture is a rich ground for the propagation of shame. Television in particular exploits the individual viewer's response to what resembles an intimate shameful moment, which is aired for all to see.

As TV increasingly shows a wider range of identities and actively attends to the representation of marginalized or previously excluded groups, it allows for a greater circulation of images of specifically gendered, sexed, and raced shame. The increased representation of groups such as women and queers now allows individuals a specific reexperience of the shame of their gender, sex, or race. While a lack of representation may have been painful, it may have been less shaming. But of course cultural representations of gays, lesbians, blacks, and more generally women were never completely absent; rather, these groups were overrepresented in terms of pathological depictions. The sad gay man, the demented housewife, and the infantilized black subject were indeed shameful representations that fueled a public knowledge and perhaps acceptance of certain forms of gendered, raced, and sexed shame. Prized moments of putative pride can also be shameful. For instance, the BBC production of Sarah Walter's novel *Tipping the Velvet* was lauded for bringing explicit representation of lesbian sex to primetime television. While many lesbians laughed at the program's dubious grasp of what constitutes their sexual practices, other viewers watched it as documentary evidence: "Oh, so that's what they do." Never mind that *Tipping the Velvet* is a fictional account of nineteenth-century London, the day after it aired conversations about the program seemed inevitably to turn to leather dildos. Or as an elderly male colleague asked me, "Is 'tipping the velvet' a metaphor . . . for . . . ?" To which I responded in an equally halting manner: "Um . . . oral sex."

In fostering the illusion of what lesbians "really do," popular representations of sexuality can provide fertile ground for the airing of shame. In regard to gay shame, Sally Munt argues that a primal shaming of queers is met again and again with public reenactments of that shame. Along with many others, Munt's project is directed at rehabilitating this shame. The queer movement in general, including queer theory, has attempted to replace sexed shame with sexual pride.[22] Munt emphasizes the link between queer politics and the overturning of shame: "gay identity as a desirable (no longer shamed) commodity" produces "modalities of shame-avoidance."[23]

> An "I" and a "we" emerge . . . from the double-valenced interstices of shame. Shame then has a contradictory latency; on the one hand, it can reinforce conformity, and on the other it can liberate new grammars of gender which emerge in pride, shame's corollary.[24]

While it's hard not to laud these new grammars, Munt's depiction of shame tends to generalize about who or what constitutes shame's object. Munt is "reminded that in classical Western culture shame is discursively linked to women, and to be 'passively' receptive to anal sex is associated with femininity and non-citizenship."[25]

WHO IS THE SHAMER?

If Munt sees shame as linked to women, she doesn't suggest that women or queers might be better at shaming others. This wouldn't necessarily contradict her argument, although it might compromise her insistence on pride. After all, if historically women and queers have been made to feel ashamed and as a consequence have become more attuned to detecting the shame of others, it makes a certain sense that the subordinated may have more nuanced skills at shaming than the privileged. The common sense of this proposition is evidenced in shaming slogans used by queers and feminists: from the queer epithet "breeders," directed at straights (and indeed the appellation "straight"), to the more complex equations familiar to feminism, such as "porn is the theory, rape the practice" and "a woman needs a man like a fish needs a bicycle." Despite all this, the idea of being a shamer is not widely and enthusiastically circulated in queer and feminist circles. Of course, a nicer view of shaming is the accepted wisdom that women have acted as a civilizing agent throughout history, from colonial settlement to the inclusion of girls in previously all-male schools and colleges.

The concept of shaming's role in the good society has been most developed in the work of John Braithwaite, an Australian criminologist. His 1989 book, *Crime, Shame, and Reintegration,* marked a decisive turn in criminology and subsequently in policing practice. Braithwaite's output is prodigious. Despite his intentions, his work has also inspired some rather dubious practices; for example, forcing drunk drivers to wear a sandwich board to identify themselves publicly is now an accepted sentencing practice in the United States, as previously stated.

The core idea in Braithwaite's articulation of shaming is that shame can be either reintegrative or stigmatizing. It all depends on the context in which shaming takes place. Braithwaite took the idea originally from a New Zealand legal initiative that had been based on Maori traditions. It is argued that within close communities, shaming the offender works better than other more formal sanctions, because individuals care deeply about what their family and friends think about them. Braithwaite argues that the desire to be accepted by those close to us is a common aspiration of humankind: we all fear that "deviance will evoke some respect or status loss among acquaintances or in the community as a whole."[26] He cites particular societies where shaming works well, such as China, Japan, and North Africa.

Shaming's success depends on whether it produces re-integration as opposed to disintegration. As Braithwaite puts it, "Much turns on this distinction."[27] Braithwaite's ideas are underpinned by communitarian ideals, which have become more pronounced in his recent work. The capacity for inter-dependency is crucial to a good outcome of shaming, as is a context of respect. In this way, "reintegrative shaming communicates disapproval within a continuum of respect for the offender: the offender is treated as a good person who has done a bad deed."[28] A disintegrative use of shame, on the other hand, produces stigmatization and has dire consequences:

> When people shame us in a degrading way, this poses a threat to our identity. One way we can deal with threat is to reject our rejecters. Once I have labeled them as dirt, does it matter that they regard me as dirt? . . . Disrespect begets disrespect. . . . I have no hope of seeking out a respected identity under your values.[29]

Braithwaite supports his argument with various examples. The Nanante ceremony in Afghanistan, for instance, features a scenario in which the offender not only meets his victims but also brings a sheep as a peace offering. The disciplinary system of the Japanese schoolroom is cited for the lengthy process conducted by teachers of communicating to the offender's parents and to other students why the offensive behavior in question must be punished.

Braithwaite's theory formed the basis for a 1991 pilot policing project in Wagga Wagga, a rural town in New South Wales. The program was called Effective Cautioning Using Family Group Conferencing—a reference to the conferencing movement, which since 1989 has been a part of New Zealand common law. It was run by local police and evaluated by criminologists at Charles Sturt, the local university. John McDonald and David Moore, directors of Transformative Justice Australia and advisers to police commissions, were involved in assessing the program. McDonald and Moore found that "the expression of shame occurs at a turning point in the conference." In line with Braithwaite's insistence on reintegrative shaming, they also found that "the offer of forgiveness can be a very important reaction—or interaction."[30]

In their recent review of the Wagga Wagga program, McDonald and Moore now argue that while the criminological theory made important predictions about what the experience of shame could do, "it said less about what shame is."[31] This led them to other theories about shame, including Tomkins's. They now argue strongly that the success of conferencing lies not in the individual offender's admission of shame but in the collective experience of the conference:

> The affect auxiliary of shame is essentially a brake on the positive affects of interest and enjoyment (or relief). Thus, there is a neutral aspect to this collective experience: shame is an absence of the positive, rather than something negative in its own right. And there is even a positive aspect to the experience. The collective experience and expression of shame is a visceral reminder: participants can experience positive emotions in each other's company.[32]

McDonald and Moore's account offers a much-needed grounding to some of Braithwaite's more general claims. Their application here is admittedly narrow in its focus on community conferencing programs, but their attention to "*what* is happening rather than *why*" is salutary.[33]

Braithwaite's argument is, per force, at another level of abstraction. It aims, after all, to be a theory rather than a manual for shaming. If some of the detail drops out about the "what" and the "why," it is still pretty interesting. Statements such as "shaming gives socialization content" or "we all need a refresher course in the consequences of a compromised conscience" whet the appetite for detail.[34] Equally, his ideas on gender, or more precisely on the role women play in shaming, are interesting but abstract. Guided by his commitment to communitarian thinking, he argues that women rarely commit serious crimes because "the female is always more socially integrated." Positioned within rather than outside social systems, "females will more often be the objects and instruments of reintegrative shaming."[35] In his description, living in patriarchal society means that women go from one set of interdependencies to another (from family to marriage). Within these structures women are socialized by reintegrative shaming and then become adept at using it to socialize others. Boys, on the other hand, are given the freedom of "time out" from the family. They are also more likely to be the objects of stigmatization. Boys, according to Braithwaite, will more often be thrown out of the home. And it will be the fathers who banish their sons outright, whereas mothers will seek to reintegrate their sons into the family by shaming them into good behavior.

In this description we might query whether the father's banishment of the son embodies an affect other than shame, such as disgust or contempt. The mother's action is clearly bound by the desire not to lose the object of interest, and her use of shame instigates only a temporary break in communication.

As a generalized system of justice, shaming has also been the object of serious critique.[36] Harry Blagg, a criminologist in Western Australia, contends that Braithwaite's model suffers from its basis in "bed-rock of consensus," and his thesis "may not have the universality claimed by its proponents."[37] Blagg's critique is particularly interesting because his argument against the universalism that underlies the model returns it to Braithwaite's starting point—Indigenous New Zealand. Maori society, according to Blagg, cannot be used to draw general conclusions, especially not with regard to other indigenous societies. Although shaming does appear to work within a Maori context, it is because of the highly structured, hierarchical society. It works in spite of, rather than because of, its appropriation by white administrators. From the anthropological literature, in many indigenous societies, "'reputation' has a certain autonomous life which leads to 'a concern for repute, both as a sentiment but also as the public recognition of that sentiment.'"[38]

Blagg is especially concerned with how reintegrative shaming is put into practice within Aboriginal contexts. He points out that, given the degradation most Aboriginal Australians contend with on a daily basis, the idea of being shamed by a police-led conferencing group is laughable.[39] Blagg's critique suggests that shaming within the justice system may not have the desired effect on those who systematically have been the objects of historical shaming. This much is pretty obvious: if you and your people have been the object of governmental practices that seek to devalue any sense of self and culture, why would you care if those authorities, or the wider society they represent, do not have regard for you? And if shaming does work within the close-bonded network of friends and family, it's a different matter altogether when shame is wielded by unknown bodies of white authority.

To be fair, Braithwaite and his followers recognize this point. Braithwaite's underlying communitarianism places much hope on a conception of individuals and society in which respect and interdependency are integrated. As he states, "Shaming is more than just when bonds of respect are maintained."[40] Not only does shaming require an a priori network of respect, but also wrongly used it may destroy respect. In the case of already damaged individuals, shaming may be lethal. In this regard, Braithwaite recounts an episode that served as inspiration for his model and also chillingly speaks of how far wrong shaming can go.

The example comes from his father, who was a prisoner of war in Borneo after the fall of Singapore in 1942. Living in absolutely degrading conditions, the prisoners nonetheless had a strict system of honor. They were paid a pittance for their work, and, having nowhere safe to keep their money, the men kept it near their beds. At one point some money went missing. One of the men was suspected and tried in a kangaroo court. Found guilty, he was sent to Coventry. As Braithwaite recounts it, the physical abuse of the camp and the emotional anguish of being rejected by his fellow prisoners proved too much, and the young man died. After his death, the other men happened upon a rat's nest, where lo and behold they found the missing money.

Braithwaite takes this tale to heart and states that the impetus of his book "has been about the power of shaming to do good."[41] Obviously, his father's story affected him greatly. It's the only time that a sense of the viscerality of shame interrupts his argument. An added detail makes it even more gripping. On their return, the soldiers had to face the relatives of the dead man. Braithwaite doesn't say what this experience did to his father or indeed what effect that living in the shadow of such deep shame may have had on his own childhood. His use of this example seems to concentrate on the moment the man presumed to be a thief is shamed. But it is impossible to read it without thinking about the shame experienced by the soldiers who had to live with the memory of their mate's death, caused in part by their actions.

Obviously, Braithwaite would be aware of this aspect of shame. In reaction to his father's shame, he has evolved an unshakable belief in the power of human good, one that transcends material situations that threaten to undo it. While this is mostly unsaid, he argues strongly that his model rejects bad uses of shame. He ends with an argument against an indiscriminate use of shame: such a society would "inevitably use its power to shame both rapists and homosexuals." Against bad uses of shaming, Braithwaite holds that "the realm of political choice, of conflict, of human agency" will decide its appropriate use.[42] From this discussion of shame within the justice system, I now turn to the use of shame more broadly within the public sphere. As a concrete instance of good shaming at work, Braithwaite cites feminism's power to make men respect new laws about sexual harassment and rape. In terms of their gender, women are positioned in his model as informed by reintegrative shaming and are experienced as good shamers in wielding their powers. While feminism may be an instance of good shaming, Braithwaite doesn't discuss how those who are the object of feminist shame will feel.

From the example I cited earlier, it's clear some people take shaming badly. From the backlash Web site example of the man who sees men being shamed all around him, one senses not reintegration but stigmatization. More generally, the backlash movement sees itself as whipped by the symbolic power that feminism supposedly deploys. "They've made us—men—feel bad about ourselves" might be a common complaint. In this refrain we hear echoes of Braithwaite's claim that "shaming is more pregnant with symbolic content than punishment [is]."[43] It is, however, felt by *some* as punishment.

Clearly what emerges from the above discussion is that some uses of shame can close down the possibilities for better social organization. Shame can serve to produce and police a certain morality that lends itself to the desire for codification. It really depends on where you think shame comes from and whether it is considered "bad" from the outset. If, as I've argued, shame is intrinsic to humankind, then it's hard to conceive of how we would get rid of it. And if you think the shame response alerts us to the presence of another and attunes us to our actions in the world, it's hard to see why we would want to get rid of it. However, if shame is construed only as a means of reproach and becomes a way of wielding power under the guise of moral rectitude, its uses are likely to be unpalatable. Moreover, for those groups who have born the brunt of this type of insidious power, shame is something to be feared.

SHAME ON THE NATION

Let me now explore these ideas in a more concrete way. I want to raise the differences and the connections between personal feelings of shame and a wider politics of shame and shaming. The following example focuses on white feminist shame—primarily my own—but it also concerns public declarations of being ashamed. The site where my shame as a white feminist ignited was the Australian Reconciliation Convention. Held in May 1997 in Melbourne, it coincided with the thirtieth anniversary of the referendum that, according to the convention's program, was to "bring about basic human rights for Australia's indigenous peoples." Organized by the Aboriginal Reconciliation Council, then headed by Patrick Dodson, the convention was a nodal point that brought together nearly two thousand whites and blacks, leaders and ordinary individuals. It took place at a time when the Australian nation was fractured by competing accounts of the past, with little political vision of the future.[44] Not that much has changed since then, although certain prominent personages, such as the leader of the right-wing and openly xenophobic One Nation Party,[45] have departed from the political main stage.

The convention coincided with the publication of *Bringing Them Home: The Report of the National Inquiry into the Separation of Aboriginal and Torres Strait Islander Children from Their Families*.[46] This inquiry took evidence from 535 Indigenous people about their experience of the government policies that forcibly removed thousands of Indigenous children from their families, commonly called the Stolen Generations. In the words of the inquiry, the laws, practices, and policies that continued into the 1970s were dedicated to the removal and the genocidal eradication of the Indigenous people of Australia.[47]

It's not quite true that the Australian political climate hasn't changed since 1997. Interest levels in Reconciliation have dropped off. The Reconciliation Council has dissolved, big events have occurred such as the war with Iraq and the bombings in Bali, and whites are impatient with the continuing problem of Aboriginal people dying twenty years younger than the rest; interest seems to have turned elsewhere.

But let's get back to the convention. It was held in the big and somewhat bland Melbourne Exhibition and Convention Centre. For all the solemnity of the occasion, the space buzzed with excitement. Groups of Aboriginal people gathered and then went off and then came together again. After sitting on the floor or in the uncomfortable chairs, they would go for

a smoke or to say hi to a friend. Conference delegates met
up with friends and family they hadn't seen in a while. The
Aboriginals looked with respect at their elders, who moved
around shyly. Younger leaders in suits or casual clothes were
surrounded by journalists. The place hummed.

It was all brand new to me. I was there with my girlfriend
at the time, a white woman who had been involved in many
political scenes in Australia. She knew the protocol better than
I did. I just wanted to stare or, conversely, fade away. I felt very
white. The fairness of some of the Aboriginal people made me
feel all the whiter. Lines of knowing and ignorance engulfed
me: who was Aboriginal, who was not, who knew whom,
which were the "good" groups. I wanted to sit invisibly in a
corner. At the same time I wanted to be a part of those groups
of Aboriginal women talking so animatedly, with such intelligence. Occasionally, I'd see the familiar faces of women from
my university. I'd smile. I know that smile when I don't know
where to put myself. It's more of a grimace. In any case they
were busy. They didn't have the time (or worse, the interest)
to smile back.

We settled into our seats in the main hall. Prime Minster
John Howard was going to address the convention. On stage
were the leaders of various groups, Indigenous and non-
Indigenous, who had sometimes fought battles together,
sometimes not. As the session began, there was talk about
Reconciliation as a people's movement. While the convention marked a moment measured out in bureaucratic time, it
seemed like a celebration too. The sheer diversity of people in
the hall attested to its specialness. Young and old, black and
white, multicultural—we were, above all, hopeful. Having
missed the 1960s and the manifestations of civil rights movements, I wondered if they had been something like this.
Excitement squeezed out cynicism. Interest crackled. It was
exhilarating. It was history.

Then, just as I was getting caught up in the process and be-

ginning to shed my awkwardness, a shift happened. The prime
minister got up to speak. His voice got louder. He got pink
and angry. What an unappealing man, I thought. Then I real-
ized with a shock that the entire room had shifted. Without a
sign, the majority of the audience had risen and turned their
backs to the stage.

I can't remember whether my girlfriend rose and did the
same. I think her body turned. I was totally caught out and
torn. Whether to rise and join ranks? Whether to sit and
gawk? I sat with my head in my hands. Cop-out or white-out:
too much going on; too much to process.

In the subsequent coverage of the convention and in relation to the Stolen Generations report, shame was everywhere.
Pronouncements of shame on the part of ordinary Australians
could be heard in letters to the editor, talk-back shows, and
literally on the street. Shame was also expressed by prominent
Australians such as the "lipstick queen," Poppy King (the
owner of a cosmetics enterprise), who declared that knowing what she now knew, she wouldn't have accepted her 1995
Australian of the Year award: "I am ashamed to say today
that I am Australian." [48] The expat Germaine Greer told an
audience in London "she would not return to Australia until
Aboriginal sovereignty was recognised" (which to many
in Australia came as a bit of a relief). [49] The minister for
Aboriginal and Torres Strait Islander Affairs at the time, John
Herron, replied: "I hate Australians going overseas and dump-
ing on our country." [50]

Was that shame? It seemed sincere, it seemed to be different from guilt. It was profoundly disturbing. It drove a wedge
between previously sanctioned ignorance and newly owned
knowledge. This played out in tortuous attempts to find the
right analogy. Where do you find the words with which to
speak a new knowledge, a new emotion? In response to the
report on the Stolen Generations, respected writers such as
Bob Ellis were tongue-tied. The analogies bred like rabbits:

to the lynchings in the American South of the 1930s, to white "victims of pederastic abuse," to "losing a pet dog and never seeing it again." He ended his column with these lines: "And I am, today, ashamed to be Australian. How about you?"[51]

In Parliament, Kim Beasley, at the time the leader of the opposition, was visibly emotional when he spoke about the report. In many regards Beasley is a bigger man than Howard. Was it shame that caused him to stutter? And what was the emotion that caused one letter writer to the *Sydney Morning Herald* to state: "That a man of his proportions could stand there and choke on his words was appalling"?[52] And what was it that prompted another to write in against the "fat-ist" nature of that remark?

One of Sedgwick's aphorisms is that "people are different." Mine is that people are weird. When I think back to that period following the convention and the report, it felt like we whites were twisting in the wind. Perhaps more aptly, we were acting out, to use the psychoanalytic term to describe wild and unproductive behavior. It's hard to read at a distance exactly which affects were being felt. There may have been some fear-terror and maybe some anger-rage. No doubt there was interest and excitement about the possibility of a new phase of politics. Without question, a range of affects were at play, and they may even have been at odds with the emotions expressed. However, we need to take at face value the public statements. These are social expressions of emotion, even as they get blurred or channeled into both predictable and unreadable political directions. As Sedgwick writes, the "psychological operations of shame, denial, projection around 'ignorance' produce pulsations of wild energies."[53]

The Reconciliation Convention and the Stolen Generation report sparked shame at an intersection of ignorance and knowledge and rendered obvious and painful the nature of white relations to Indigenous Australians. It was very much a moment of white shame—it felt white-hot, and it could not be ignored. Of course the events were extraordinary, and they allowed for white ignorance to be accepted (by other whites) as extraordinary. But nothing new was really said. No information was released that could have been new to people, that they could not have known about for some time. Many would have had firsthand knowledge of the forced abduction of Aboriginal children, and others would have heard tales from their parents and grandparents. So why did the convention and the report cause such an outpouring of shame? Certainly the facts and figures made for painful reading, but the public acceptance of shame allowed people to own up to their ignorance. As such, shame allowed for knowledge to circulate, softened by the affective cloaking of shared emotions.

A film was made in 2002 that focused on one story of abduction. *Rabbit-Proof Fence* was written by Doris Pilkington, the daughter of a woman who had been stolen. The "true story" concerns three Aboriginal sisters who run away from the mission school where they have been placed after being taken from their family, and they follow a rabbit-proof fence over a thousand miles back to their home. The director of the film, Phil Noyce, is clear about his strategy: "Stolen children stories can be so painful you can't bear them. But this story is a triumph. It shows their extraordinary spirit." He places the film in the learning curve initiated by Reconciliation events:

> With other films, you have to stimulate people's interest. With this one, it felt Australia actually wanted a vehicle that would allow them to get closer to understanding things that happened in the past. So many of us have a suppressed relationship with Aboriginal Australia. . . . By emotionally affecting people, I hope it helps them to understand.[54]

Compared with the hard facts in the report, Noyce's film lets us face our ignorance and shame in a less confronting way. In an interview in the *Observer* prior to the film's opening in the United Kingdom, Noyce offers this reading of the film's popularity in Australia:

It says that white Australians needed a vehicle to express this huge shift that everyone made. And I think that Australians were just longing for that, longing to celebrate their alternative history, longing to celebrate these women, longing to come out of ignorance. And, ultimately, longing to celebrate their blackness.[55]

"Longing to come out of ignorance." While Noyce may overstate the nature of the shift, it's undeniable that the film touched those who had somehow managed to remain outside the previous debate. One could critique the film for offering an easy way out of ignorance, but it's dangerous to dismiss people's emotional grappling with tough issues. Expressions of shame, whether promoted by the *Bringing Them Home* report or in relation to *Rabbit-Proof Fence,* opened the way for a momentary reckoning. As Sedgwick argues, the task is then "to pluralize and specify" the ignorance that the public was forced to contend with. She elaborates on the need to acknowledge a "plethora of *ignorances,* and . . . the labor, erotics, and economics of their human production and distribution."[56] I'd add that this task has to be undertaken affectively and with emotion, rather than through moral lectures by those who would set themselves apart from the emotional fray.

INCOMMENSURABILITIES

How did white women handle that moment of white shame? Women were prominent within many of the white community organizations represented at the Australian Reconciliation Convention. The grassroots expression of shame came from women all over the country. Following the convention, they found many ways to demonstrate shame: the Sorry Books that sprang up, the sea of hands that waved across the land, the apologies from local councils, churches, and educational groups. All these actions used the feelings of shame to overcome impotence. Shame became a prompt for action. As Chris

Cunneen argues, these actions were aimed at "providing *both* moral and political leverage."[57]

Similarly, queers expressed outrage along with shame. They directed anger into the formation of Aboriginal and non-Aboriginal coalitions such as Black + White + Pink, a powerful campaign against racism, homophobia, and violence. They set up Queers for Reconciliation. They built floats to protest the government's refusal to say sorry and paraded down Oxford Street in the Sydney Gay and Lesbian Mardi Gras. These groups remain important as activist organizations.

Where the queer groups diverge substantially from some parts of feminism is their unwillingness to speak on behalf of others. It's a tricky thing not to do, despite years of caution and critique. The imperative not to represent in a colonizing manner the feelings and fears of others is especially difficult in highly charged emotional times. How do you voice your own shame *and* a collective one without shaming again the objects of that shame? When statements shift from "I am ashamed" to "we are ashamed," important distinctions emerge. The movement from the first-person singular to the collective inaugurates a very different deployment of shame's effects. "I am ashamed" demands some recognition of one's intricate involvement within a shaming moment; it requires a pause and reflection on what has provoked the shame response. Ideally, it provokes some level of consideration about where and how a connection based in interest has been broken. "We are ashamed," however, can quickly become the cry of one group against another, wherein the intricacy of shame is lost. As soon as it becomes a rallying call, the potential for reflection diminishes. There are, of course, instances when the individual voices combine without losing their distinctness—when individual reflection is fed by collective reckoning. And that's the trick in public uses of shame. How can shame be used not as moral reproach but as a goad for action?

In Australian feminism, as in feminism elsewhere, white shame focusing on Indigenous women has been notably used in order to shame white women. White feminist indignation too often uses the bodies of nonwhite women as an alibi. For instance, in an infamous moment in Australian feminism, a white anthropologist, apparently feeling compelled to speak out against rape in Aboriginal communities, asked a question that didn't really belong to her. In an article published in 1999, Diane Bell, in an accusing manner, directed this question in the main to white feminists: "Who speaks of the anguish, shame and risk for the Indigenous woman?"[58] The gist of her argument was that rape is indigenous to all women.[59] While she may well have acted in good faith, the manner and mode of address were wrong, especially in regard to Aboriginal protocol. In Aboriginal English, she performed a "shame job," which is to say she singled herself out from the group in a way that brought shame on herself and the group. The "Bell debate" caused an immense amount of recrimination within white feminism and, more important, between white and Aboriginal women.[60] Aileen Moreton-Robinson, an Aboriginal scholar, reviews the situation in these terms: "The female body is not the site of empathy or unity between all women."[61]

Moreton-Robinson's groundbreaking book *Talkin' Up to the White Woman* is a clear exposition of the dynamics of feminist knowledge and ignorance in postcolonial societies. She argues that white feminism often takes its knowledge of Aboriginal women from white sources, dictated by white concerns. In other words, we build our knowledge in shameful ways; then, to compound the shame, we hide our ignorance behind that stolen knowledge. In Moreton-Robinson's words:

> In seeking to analyze and explain the role and status of Indigenous women, women anthropologists have sought to investigate how their cultural spheres are in substance unlike or like those of their white sisters, through the centering of their analyses on the areas of concern to white feminist discourse.[62]

Moreton-Robinson supports her argument with interviews she conducted with white academic feminists in Australia. Some of the responses weren't pretty. In the words of one:

> Let me just say this straight—you get beaten up a lot—you get beaten up for being racist—not in the physical sense—but verbally beaten up and of course you get pissed off because, you know, I am really trying—why won't they accept that I am really trying! . . . Oh God, we will never get it right; it doesn't matter what we do. You know what I mean?[63]

It's important to note that Moreton-Robinson is not telling white women to stop trying to counter their racism and that of others. I hope this frustrated woman has kept on trying to "get it right."

In the white woman's exasperated cry of "we will never get it right," one can hear the desire to take the easier road. It's understandable, as in Lehtinen's argument, that we use subordination as a ground that connects us all and allows us empathy in shame. Shame violently affects our sense of our self. It's understandable that we seek to share our shame in order to alleviate that intensely painful feeling. A sense of that temptation to connect in the name of shame can be heard in a poem by Paula Gunn Allen called "Some Like Indians Endure."

> i have it in mind that
> dykes are indians
>
> . . .
>
> indian is an idea
> some people have
> of themselves
> dyke is an idea some women
> have of themselves
> the place where we live now
> is idea

because whiteman took
all the rest
. . .
so dykes
are like indians
because everyone is related
to everyone
in pain
in terror
in guilt
in blood
in shame
in disappearance
that never quite manages
to be disappeared
we never go away
even if we're always
leaving.[64]

The poem engages us so beautifully. The connection of our bodies carried through terror, guilt, blood, and shame bonds us at a visceral level. In the face of the shame, guilt, and remorse that white feminists may feel individually, the desire to reach for the connection this poem offers is understandable. That Paula Gunn Allen, a Laguna Pueblo/Sioux poet and a former professor of Native American studies, proffers this connection between Indians and dykes is a testimony to her intellectual and political generosity. It would, however, be a travesty of that generosity if whites were to take advantage of it instead of hearing a challenge to interrogate the grounds for connection.

Moreton-Robinson would argue the existence of profound incommensurabilities between white and Indigenous women that radically disturb the possibility of connection. She places these incommensurabilities at the heart of different embodied epistemologies:

Indigenous women as embodiments of racial difference can never know what it is like to experience the world as a white woman, just as white women can never know what it is like to experience the world as an Indigenous woman. *To know* an Indigenous constructed social world you must experience it from within; to *know about* such a world means that you are imposing a conceptual framework from outside.[65]

Her argument is a challenge on several counts. For white women it means that we need to clarify what our shame is about and what we need to do with it. It also seems to say that ignorance between whites and the Indigenous is a fact of life. More productively, it also indicates the immense amount of interest that flows between the two groups—not always pleasurable interest, but interest nonetheless. Does that mean that shame will also always be a part of the public realm in Australia and in other colonized countries? Would this be a bad thing? It depends greatly on how we understand shame and what we do with it. Returning to my previous distinctions, we might say that the affective physical level of shame alerts us to the fact we are feeling and to the facts of our feelings. At this level it is productive. The social expression of shame in the public sphere has another logic and raises other concerns. It is here that grassroots actions and other interventions in public debates are crucial. Small and large responses, big and little shames, help keep interest alive. Shame has the task of making that interest urgent.

Shame also reminds us that getting along together in a better and more equitable way is hard work. No easy connections can be made across the gulf of different experiences and histories. Shame works at a bodily level to open and close lines of connection: shame is a switching point rerouting the dynamics of knowing and ignorance. But unlike empathy, shame does not permit any automatic sharing of commonality; rather, it poses deep limits to communication. This marking of incommensurability may, however, produce localized action, reconciliation performed in local realities, bringing the past into the present. It certainly produces interest that overwhelms the possibility of remaining in ignorance. Shame thus can be used to initiate what Sedgwick calls "a fight not against originary ignorance, nor for originary ignorance, but against the killing pretence that a culture does not know what it does."[66]

The Reconciliation events produced shame that posed a challenge to *learn,* and not to *know.* To return to Wendy Brown's question cited at the beginning of this chapter, it's clear that while feminism has been good at moral reproach, we need a broader and more affecting way of engaging in politics—one that is emotionally interested in people. One of the critiques I would level at some feminist uses of shame is that in wielding emotional power, we forget to be interested in those we see as our enemy. For all its normative nature, Braithwaite's use of shaming reminds us that respect is crucial. The lack of respect in so many areas of politics makes it evident that feminism is not alone in this regard. But that doesn't lessen the shameful ways in which feminism seems at times to lack interest in those who are considered outsiders, outside the cause. We need to remember that any politics not interested in those who are placed beyond its ken will continue to be a politics of shaming: a bastion of moral reproach. And that is shameful.

4

Ancestral Shame

*I*N THIS CHAPTER, I take up the idea of ancestral shame to consider how we are related to shame in the past. The term is from Nicolas Abraham and Maria Torok's psychoanalytic work, which locates shame as "'buried alive' in one's ego."[1] I use it beyond its psychoanalytic frame to explore the effects of shame over generations. Ancestral shame reminds us of how we are forged in many different relations—those of kin but also those of geography and history. These different proximities produce very particular emotional responses and affective identities, which are transgenerational as well as intercultural.

"It crosses my mind that many of us are far away from our origins, but we exist in a place that transcends geography, we exist in a place of blood and other bonds," states Australian artist William Yang. He makes this comment in the context of a piece called "Blood Links," in which he explores his family's intercultural experiences. Being gay, of Chinese ancestry, and an Australian of several generations gives Yang a particular sensitivity to shame. Focusing on same-sex relationships and interracial friendships, his work uses shame to narrate a generous sense of history. His art is informed by a particular experience of living as "different" in the proximities imposed by small communities. In his recent performance piece *Shadows*, Yang portrays two seemingly incomparable stories: one about an extended Aboriginal family in rural New South Wales and the other about families of German ancestry living in South Australia. Both tell of exclusion from mainstream white Australian society. The German families came to Australia before World War I and, as happened elsewhere, were ostracized during World War II. They were blamed for what their relations were doing in the homeland and made to feel ashamed of being German, although any direct connection had been severed generations earlier.

Yang has developed an artistic style that mixes photography and oral stories. He describes how there is "a natural tendency to explain while showing slides as in the living room slide shows." He also acknowledges that in artistic circles, this style has "a terrible reputation," presumably because it seems so amateur. But equally, the arrangement of visual material and stories makes for a genre that embraces "large social issues, yet [is] quite intimate."[2]

Yang's work continually crosses social issues and intimate histories. Sometimes, as in *Shadows,* the issue is clearly public—the challenge of effecting reconciliation between Indigenous and non-Indigenous Australia. Sometimes, as in the recounting of the history of gay and lesbian Sydney *(Friends of Dorothy),* Yang explicitly "exposes" himself. He admits it's a hard and potentially shameful experience ("I'm not an extroverted person") but argues that "it is the role of artists to expose themselves."[3]

Whether recounting the stories of Aboriginal families, those of his own family's assimilation, or the stories of AIDS and death in Sydney, Yang sees his mission as giving "subcultural tribes . . . kindred spirits voice."[4] The emphasis is on crossing different histories and putting himself into the stories of different "tribes." This way of making sometimes shameful stories and narratives of shame finds an echo in literary/academic work on what is called transethnic relations.

The term is from Édouard Glissant, who explores the experience of being métis (hybrid), of mixed Caribbean and

French ancestry. *Transethnic relation* refers to "relation" both
as relative and as relating, or narrating. In *Poetics of Relation,*
Glissant uses relation to investigate errant movement and exile
within colonial and postcolonial situations. Like Yang, the
point is to make stories of exile more intimate, to make them
matter to the present. Glissant uses Deleuze and Guattari's notion of the rhizome. Basically, rhizomes are plants that do not
have taproots; they send off roots laterally. Conceptually, the
rhizome prompts alternative ideas about connection.

> The image of the rhizome, prompt[s] the knowledge that
> identity is no longer completely within the root but also
> in the relation . . . because the thought of errantry is also
> the thought of what is relative, the thing relayed as well as
> related.[5]

Glissant does not disavow rootedness or people's desires for
roots: "The notion of the rhizome maintains, therefore, the
idea of rootedness but challenges that of a totalitarian root."
Against "intolerant roots," "the poetics of relation" illuminates
how "each and every identity is extended with the Other."[6]
Glissant does not hide from the violence of colonial uprootings
of people. The emphasis, however, is on how different affective
experiences of being uprooted forge new forms of relations:

> For though this experience made you, original victim
> floating toward the sea's abysses, an exception, it became
> something shared and made us, the descendants, one people
> among others. Peoples do not live on exception. Relation
> is not made up of things that are foreign but of shared
> knowledge.[7]

Glissant's use of relation foregrounds the interrelatedness
of peoples, histories, and the places in which they all collide.
Relation speaks to how we, in the present, are related intimately to histories: quite literally we are relatives, we are the
descendants, says Glissant. Some of us experience the past in

relation to the emotions of the "original victims," and some in relation to the original oppressors. But this is not a taproot genealogy of familial connection.

Equally, reexperiencing the shame of the past does not have to be through blood: modes of relating to history can produce intimate connections, not unlike those of kith. Our relating to past emotions and affects moves rhizomatically; traveling along familial lines, it sparks off new shoots.

Yang's image of "blood and other bonds" places shame within the twisted geographies of the familial and historical stories of migration and within the desire and interest to relate to those histories in different ways. Of course, some families do not or will not talk of their shameful relations. There may be families without skeletons in their closet—families that never moved, never knew of anything unlike themselves. In societies like Canada and Australia, however, such radical hermeticism is nigh on impossible. These are nations forged in transethnic bonds, however much that has been denied. Contact, violent or not, is the rule and the premise of their individual and national histories.

Gershen Kaufman, a noted psychoanalyst, argues that "the examination of various intergroup dynamics from the perspective of affect . . . will yield a new theory of ethnic, racial, religious, gender, and sexual identity development." Kaufman states that "all experience becomes amplified by affect or emotion," which he says takes specific and discrete forms.[8] Analysis must attend to the various ways of relating that highlight how, at different times, different people come together through the force of collective and individual history. Those histories take on detail and color when we think about them in terms of emotion. Exploring affective relations, we can perhaps move closer to Paul Rabinow's vision of "an ethos of micro-interdependencies, with an acute consciousness of the inescapabilities and particularities of places, characters, historical trajectories and fates."[9] In what follows, I'll use an instance of ancestral shame. It concerns my own family, but the stories are public and personal. Focusing on a historical moment, I'll try to relate the different aspects of that shame: to echo Benjamin, shame is social and personal.

ONLY RELATE

Stories begin at different points, and I'll start this one in the middle. The scene is set in my bedroom. A new lover and I are in bed talking. We've since broken up, which may or may not be integral to my continuing desire to tell this story. (Well, yes, it is . . .) There we are, talking about family and about whiteness. We lie across its dividing line. She is Aboriginal and also relates to her Irish working-class background. I'm white and have a mongrel-class background.

She calls me blue (that Australian term for fair-haired), and I, surprised, say at least she's got a real white girl—that freckled and blue whiteness of redheads. It's not a shade of whiteness I like. But she doesn't seem to mind. She laughs at something I say and tells me, "You're talking Koori now." I redden and admit to putting on accents as easily as clothing. I am after all a mid-Atlantic bastard living in Australia, and my tongue loves long *a*'s: *ma-a-a-te.* She teaches me the meaning of shame in Aboriginal English: the shame of calling attention to the self (a lesson seemingly discarded in this project). I learn new phrases. "True, eh": such a comforting phrase that I want to lick it into my own vocabulary. She tells me stories; she asks me to tell mine. The stories that come easily seem inconsequential.

The story I itch to tell shames me. It's not a story from my father's side, although there are many to be told about famous forebears and their services to the British Empire. From my father I carry a surname that still signifies colonialism in parts of the world I have never visited. People occasionally come up to me at conferences and ask if I know about Probyn's Horse, a British cavalry regiment now located in Pakistan. I do, but it's not a story I identify with. The story I want to tell my lover

concerns my more enlightened Canadian maternal side—
my mother's socialist father and socially concerned mother.
I finally blurt to her, as she looks at me with calm waiting
eyes, "My grandmother was a wannabe Indian." My grandmother's poem in which she masquerades as a Native Canadian
woman—a squaw, in her words—rattles in my memory. I'm
silent before the chasm this opens. All she says is, "That's interesting, go on."

So began my interest in relating to my grandmother and
to her sense of shame, which I have reignited as my own. As
a poet, my grandmother found inspiration in those around
her. She had no problem relating to them and saw no obstacle
to relating their stories. Her acts of representation seemingly
had no guile or, to our present eyes, concern with the ethics
of representation. There were a lot of "ethnics" in her neck of
the woods, the northern interior of British Columbia, which
was one of the last Canadian frontiers. Indigenous Canadians,
Japanese, Chinese, and Doukhobor mixed with Scots, Welsh,
and some English. Going native for her seemed second nature.
In my family, jokes were told of her desire. We suspected that
a Chinese scroll given to her and proudly displayed on the
kitchen wall said, "Bugger off, white woman." When I first
came upon her poems, I blushed at their intent. Now, on the
other side of the Pacific, I wonder at her shame and shameless-
ness, which seem to shadow mine as surely as our shared first
names and red hair—a ready combination for bright blushes.

CONTACT ZONES

I'll come to her story and her poems in a moment. Of my own
experience of relating her story, I won't say much more, except
that it represents what I call an encounter within the contact
zone. The contact zone seems like an abstract idea, but it is
continually reenacted in everyday life: bedrooms can be contact zones, as can streets, libraries, shops and pubs, classrooms,
and workplaces. They are the spaces where different people

come together—where, for various reasons, they are forced into proximity. Of course, throughout history those encounters have often been painful and marked by unequal relations of power. But, as my girlfriend also made me acknowledge in her relatedness to her Irish and Aboriginal blood, sometimes the contact has been gentle and even romantic. Sex can remake the contact zone in pleasure, just as it can allow history and violence to penetrate.

In her definition of the contact zone, Mary Louise Pratt describes it as the space "where subordinated or marginal groups select and invent from materials transmitted to them by a dominant or metropolitan culture."[10] Pratt's wonderful book *Imperial Eyes* uses travel writing to analyze how the contact zone produces embodied ways of being in relation to particular geographical and historical contexts. She takes the idea of contact from linguistic studies of how languages are improvised when different peoples need to communicate in order to trade. The need to communicate makes humans very inventive. People talk to each other even when they don't like or have reason to fear the other. Contact, while often forced, has "interactive and improvisational dimensions." As a concept, the contact zone questions what happens when people "were previously separated by geographical and historical disjunctures, and [their] trajectories now intersect."[11] Pratt elaborates:

> A "contact" perspective emphasizes how subjects are constituted in and by their relations to each other. It treats relations among colonizers and colonized, or travelers and "travelees," not in terms of separateness or apartheid, but in terms of copresence, interaction, interlocking understandings and practices, often within radically asymmetrical relations of power.[12]

In this way, the contact zone focuses on the material conditions and the types of formal and informal interaction produced through them. It asks what types of relations between individuals become available and how, in local circumstances, they are reworked as the basis for transethnic interrelations. The contact zone goes against any idea of an authentic, purely indigenous or local subjectivity. It highlights the actual configurations of contact: where, when, how, and with what effects it was initiated. Contact is always both originary and ongoing. It opens discussion of how bodies within the contact zone are continually reworked in relation to specific times, histories, places, and other bodies. Dwelling on these zones of interaction rather than on conflict lends a more humane touch. This is not to seek absolution for the deeds our forebears may or may not have committed, may or may not have suffered. But it is to insist on the intimate human relations that we, the offspring of contact, continue to share.

The emphasis on relatedness and the act of relating contained within notions of transethnic relation and the contact zone is important to this task of understanding how we are related to one another. This perspective questions again, with some urgency, what it means to be human—that tricky admixture of the universal and the particular. As Clifford Geertz put it years ago, cultural analysis too easily loses "touch with the hard surfaces of life—with the political, economic, stratifactory realities within which men are everywhere contained—and with the biological and physical necessities on which those surfaces rest."[13]

For me, the emotion and affect of shame necessarily connect the hard surfaces of life and its biological and physical necessities. Too often accusations and denials of shame construct two subsets of history, that of the oppressor and the oppressed, in such a way that they cannot meet up. In other words, instead of focusing on the necessarily intertwined and intersubjective production of shame, an abstract use of the term—as in "the shameful past"—poses two solitudes, placed within the transhistorical and undifferentiated space of the shamed and the ashamed. If shame highlights what it means to be human, we need ways of using and relating to shame that make our history more humane: stories of individual and collective aspiration, fragility, and humiliation.

RELATIONS RELATING

My grandmother's story is one instance of relating within the contact zone. I call it her story, but it is also mine. My shame has brought us together in strange ways. I use our relation partly to explore how one relates to emotional expressions removed from their temporal and physical space. Here is a poem written by Elspeth Honeyman Clarke.

> I have lost her, my daughter, and never
> As long as this body may love
> Shall I see her again. In this body
> She grew, and I bore her with gladness
> And fed her with pride. I was young then,
> And death had not taken my husband,
> But death is a blow one can bear.
> If my life has been hard since her coming,
> No one knew, least of all my Elaine;
> And all that the Sisters had taught me,
> And all I could gather from reading,
> Late at night, tho' I slept as I read,
> I taught her, and sweetly she grew.
> I brushed her soft hair with a rapture
> Too keen for delight; it was fair
> Like her father's and shone in the sunlight,
> And she wore but the finest of muslins,
> With lace that the Sisters had made me
> At the neck and the hem. So time passed
> And I saw her one day as a maiden,
> Slender, dark-eyed and proud as a queen.
>
> Then she left me to go to the city
> And train as a nurse; it seemed best.

And at home I worked harder than ever
For the pretty things every girl longs for,
To hold up her head with the rest.
The nights were the worst, but the body
Must sleep, if it's worn out, at last.
I never went near her, I could not;
But for two golden weeks every summer
She came back as a child to our cottage,
And seemed glad of its shelter and peace.
I brushed her soft hair every evening,
And watched her sleep, fresh as a flower,
And my heart could not hold all its joy.

Graduation,—I sent her a trinket
And all I could spare for her flowers.
They told me her room could not hold them,
Later on, when I went there to ask—
To ask, for June came, and she came not,
Nor the next, nor any month after.
And all my blood was burnt up with my longing,
And fear, like a knife, stabbed my soul.

Still she came not. At last I could stay here
No longer. I dressed myself slowly,
Thinking, so might she wish me to look,
Though I knew no mere garment could alter
The face of a squaw, such as I.
In the hospital office they told me
She had gone long before, and they gave
An address. There they gave me another
Till at last in a row of bright houses
In a suburb, I found her. My knock
Mocked the pounding that throbbed in my side,
And she came. Her face froze when she saw me,
Then she asked what I wanted. "Elaine!"
But she answered, too loudly, "No baskets,

No thank you, no baskets today."
And I saw through the door a white table,
And flowers, and a young man's fair head,
Before the door closed on "No baskets,
No thank you, no baskets today."

She is gone. Aie—aie! I am lonely.
There is nothing in life or in death
For me now. God be good to her only,
And spare her this pain, my Elaine.

At first reading, the poem seemed very dated. Certainly no one would now entitle a poem "Half Breed."

Elspeth Honeyman Clarke died when I was very young. The name Elspeth is reasonably unusual, and when people ask me about it, I proudly reply that it was my grandmother's name. It's a bit childish to be proud of one's name. As a child I was given a pretty diminutive that was, to me, much less exotic than my real name. I have only one photograph of my grandmother, flanked by her stern-looking parents. The photograph forms the basis of my memory of her. My mother once found a tarnished lock of her once-golden hair. I could see that her hair was like mine, but I didn't like the idea of dead hair and that someday someone might come across mine lying in such a box. The first thing I did when I moved away from home was to cut off and dispose of my flowing tresses of reddish-gold hair.

When I was born my grandmother wrote a poem for me that I still have. It's written on now-faded blue writing paper and addressed "To Elspeth P from Elspeth C." It's short, the handwriting cramped. "Nourish her, and cherish her; Name her stately / —Goddess, queen, most beautiful—None so dear as she!" I don't think she wrote poems when my brother and sister were born. She didn't like the order of the names given to my brother—his initials spelled ASP, an ominous combination apparently. She gave my mother five dollars to get his name changed by deed poll. My mother didn't, and another complaint was laid at my grandmother's feet.

I'm not sure why my mother gave me a box of her mother's poems. My mother died before I published my first book, but maybe she hoped I would be a writer, like my grandmother. My mother had wanted to be a writer and to write a biography of her mother. I still have that box of poems—a battered Vyella shirt box filled with mainly undated and unreferenced pieces of writing. Some, such as "Half Breed," are typed; others are in a published form, but no one thought to mark dates on the now-yellowed paper. Several clippings are from local newspapers, which occasionally note that the poem was reprinted from the *New York Times*.

In the box, I found an unidentified newspaper article that describes my grandmother:

> This thoroughly normal woman does not go about swapping soulful strophes with other poets and addressing societies. Quite the contrary. For many years her husband's profession of a civil engineer led her into the far and wilder parts of the province, living in tents and wikiups where, with real pioneer spirit she undertook the education of her two children from matter supplied by the department of education at Victoria, and made a good job of it.

Many of her poems try to capture the beauty of the land through which my grandfather was building roads. She wrote the lyrics for a song that had some success. The sheet music is part of the collection. It looks very grand, printed by Arthur H. Stockwell, Ltd., of Ludgate Hill EC4. A friend comments on the intricacy of the melody and the fact that it is in B minor, an off key, which is unusual in the genre of frontier tunes for the amateur musician. Called "The Cariboo Trail," the cover drawing comes straight from an Englishman's romantic ideas of the frontier. It's land that my grandfather was efficiently paving over.

Both my grandparents were socialists and atheists who

refused to baptize their children, something my mother later
found shameful when she remained in her pew while we
trooped up for communion. Her poems are strongly imprinted
with liberal humanism and concern issues of social justice.
She was known to befriend ethnic workers. There is also a now
long forgotten tale of her brother marrying an Indigenous
woman. I don't know if they all got on well together. For her
time, she seems to have been socially aware. She was a devoted
Anglophile in cultural matters, and in later years my grandparents collected great stacks of the *Manchester Guardian*.

In other poems, I catch snippets of her affective relationship to the land and a pronounced relation to loss—of land,
and of love.

> Cry of loons across the lake—
> Should a heart that's mended, ache?
> ("Resolution")

The cry of the loons, the rain that beats upon the house
that shuts in, keeps safe, keeps out, reproaches, reminds of
impossible wishes:

> Sharp needle-pointed rain
> Striking the window-pane,
> Breaking the silence,
> Stabs heart and brain.
> ("Rain")

There's a constant ache that the country won't quite let her
in, that existence will always be fitful; it will always coexist
with layers of the dead, the disappeared:

> Lady, if beneath your pillow
> Men are lying dead,
> They would wish you peaceful slumbers
> In your narrow bed.
> ("Song of the Rails")

But what of that first long poem I cited? "Half Breed"—
it's a blunt and direct title. When I first read the poem I was
struck by a vicarious shame. "Shame can be gifted beyond
generations, sometimes bypassing verbal communication."[14]

I became obsessed with the presence of desire in her
poems—in "Half Breed"—a desire to take on, enter into, and
maybe take over the body of a Native woman. Reading the
poem again, I notice other expressions of emotion. From "feed-
ing her daughter with pride," and the wish to provide "the pretty
things every girl longs for / To hold up her head with the rest,"
to the mother's delight in her daughter's fair hair inherited from
the long-dead father, and her deferral to the authority of the
nuns, the poem is filled with depictions of the shaming gazes of
others. The shame of class: being able to afford only "trinkets";
the shame of race: "the face of a squaw, such as I"; the shame of
interracial marriage: the fair-haired, dark-eyed daughter and her
"young man's fair head." All of these pale before the shaming
gaze of the daughter, who disowns her mother: "No baskets, /
No thank you, no baskets today." And finally the forlorn hope
that her daughter be spared such pain—that Elaine's own "half
breed," mixed-race child, fathered by the young man with fair
hair, not abandon her.

The shame in the poem is easy to trace, as its sources are. In
Martha Nussbaum's terms, the shame and the pain are represented in ways that foreground the "aboutness" of the emotion.
As Nussbaum puts it, "The particular depth and the potentially
terrifying character of the human emotions derive from the
especially complicated thoughts that humans are likely to form
about their own need for objects, and about their imperfect control over them." She lists the emotions: fear, love, hope, anger,
gratitude, hatred, jealousy, pity, and guilt. These all have an
"intentional object: that is, it figures in the emotion as it is seen
or interpreted by the person whose emotion it is." In this sense,
"emotions always involve thought of an object combined with
thought of the object's salience or importance."[15]

In Nussbaum's account emotions come into being because we recognize we cannot control the object, in which we have invested so much, and this lack of control becomes integral to the emotion. This sets the scene for the emergence of "childhood emotions that are especially dangerous to morality: in particular, shame at the limitations of the body and envy of others who control what we wish to control but don't." Drawing on object-relations theory, especially Winnicott and Klein, Nussbaum describes human infancy in terms of our unique combination of early cognitive capacity with physical incapacity. Very early on we know that we are dependent on others for our survival. This cognition of our imperfection and our neediness is central to human development. We are marked, in varying ways, by that formative (and continuing) knowledge. In this, our bodies fail our intellect. Shame for Nussbaum is mired in our childhood experiences of physical dependence. She calls this "primitive shame." "A primitive shame at one's weakness and impotence is," she writes, "probably a basic and universal feature of the emotional life."[16]

In my grandmother's poem, there does seem to be something like a primal shame. The concern for the daughter evoked in the descriptions of the mother's attention is seemingly unreciprocated. Mustn't such love that goes unreturned cause shame in the mother? The neediness of the mother is then amplified unbearably by her daughter's rejection. Indeed, rejection may be too tame a word to capture the obliteration the mother experiences in her daughter's presence. The rejection of the mother is clearly a shamed response on the part of the daughter. She cannot look at her mother. Shutting the door on her, the daughter is clearly ashamed. What could her mother have done to merit such shame and humiliation?

In Nussbaum's account, the mother-daughter relationship is fraught with universal and primitive shame, based in the physical dependence that is our human condition. And in some ways, the poem does speak of this. However, the daughter's

humiliating rejection of her mother seems to spring from a less
basic experience. The daughter is, after all, a "half breed," the
result of her mother's sexual encounter with a white man. We do
not know if the sex was forced; however, the daughter's father
seems to have long disappeared. If, in general, children find the
idea of their parents having sexual intercourse embarrassing, in
the historical context, being the result of interracial sex would
produce heightened feelings of shame.

Zoë Wicomb argues that the mere evocation of interracial sex produces shame. In the context of the "new" South
Africa, she discusses the case of repatriating the body of Saarte
Baartman ("The Hottentot Venus"). Wicomb writes of "the
shame invested in those (females) who have mated with the
colonizer." As she puts it, in South Africa "we do not speak
about miscegenation; it is after all the very nature of shame
to stifle its discourse." Paraphrasing Salman Rushdie, she
concludes that "what the Baartman case shows is how shame,
cross-eyed and shy, stalks the postcolonial world broken
mirror in hand, reproducing itself in puzzling distortions."[17]
Wicomb uses the literary trope of the chiasmus to describe
the working of shame. Rhetorically, this results in "the denial
of a quality 'x' to an object or place which common sense
holds it to actually possess, with the compensating attribution to everything but that object or place."[18] Shame, in this
sense, is attributed to everyone except those who have caused
the shame. In Wicomb's analysis, "shame is identified as the
recognition of being the object of another's shame."[19] For the
products of forbidden interracial sex, one is the embodiment
of another's shame, forced to wear that shame as one's own.

At the level of physical bodies, the contact zone is the space
of miscegenation. It can't be forgotten that the copresence of
different people has produced, through sex, whether forced or
consensual, the bodies of the mixed race: the colored in South
Africa or the "fair" Indigenous. These are the very embodied
subjects of Glissant's "relatedness of the transethnic." They are

the flesh and blood of the contact zone, and, as Wicomb so
clearly demonstrates, they are still positioned as the objects of
its continuing shame: "An unacknowledged shame steeped in
its originary interracial sex . . . [produces] not a lack of identity
but shameful excess."[20]

Why did my grandmother so identify with the shame of
interracial sex? Was it the general conditions of the time, when
liaisons between white men and Indigenous women were
tacitly acknowledged? Was there a particular reason for her
identification with interracial sex? Do I have Indigenous great
aunts and cousins connected by blood if not by name? Like
many, I simply do not know, and the family connections are
now long dead. But from the grave and in the poem there is
certainly a shameful excess of identification. We can hear in
the poem the evocation of shame as a sickness of the soul. The
use of the French expression *aie* to signify pain may have been
affectation, but it's as if English couldn't reach the depths of
that pain, shame, and loneliness.

While one could excuse such attachment as based in good
intentions, Dominick LaCapra, a specialist in Holocaust
literature, is deeply critical of any easy empathetic identification with victims. He understands empathy as unsettled and
unsettling: "The other is recognized and respected as other."[21]
Empathetic unsettlement cannot be passive or accepting;
it is a practice, and maybe a duty. As he puts it, empathy
may be something like an entitlement that one has to earn.
Empathetic unsettlement entails a mode of relating that upsets
easy narrative or harmonizing narration. And this mode of
relating may be hard work and painful. LaCapra argues that
relating to history, especially traumatic parts of a common
history, should radically challenge accepted ideas. It shakes up
and forces us to reevaluate who we think we are. This position
does not allow for dispassionate distance or a "feel good" com-
munal wallowing in pain in order for catharsis and absolution
to occur. It requires a genre or style that "allows for the terse

interplay between critique, necessary objectifying reconstruction and affective response to the voices of victims."[22] While no genre or discipline owns trauma, writing, reading, or listening to affect demands "an ethics of response." Echoing the idea of shame as hauntology, LaCapra states that "the after-effects—the hauntingly possessive ghosts—of traumatic events are not fully owned by anyone." He definitively cautions against an indiscriminate generalization of trauma.[23]

It's here that shame becomes much trickier, as does the reading of my grandmother's excessive identifications. In terms of postcolonial and feminist critique, we would question the way in which she takes on the voice, experience, and body of another— the white woman representing the pain of the other, who is silenced by a history in which white women collude. In bell hooks's argument, "the desire to make contact with those bodies deemed Other, with no apparent will to dominate, assuages the guilt of the past,"[24] and she cautions us to be wary of this.

It's an important critique. But in this context it may be too general to catch the nuances of shame in the contact zone. I think hooks's argument also misses the important question of whether we can experience and deploy empathy in ways that do not obliterate the other. How do we represent these trans-ethnic relations in ways that neither deny accountability nor obscure difference through an overidentification?

To my mind, it is more interesting to apply LaCapra's reading of affect. His model emphasizes the high costs of a conflation of very different subject positions. It also foregrounds the historical conditions in which traumatic affect is produced, inflicted, and experienced, and it demands that present-day readers place themselves in relation to that history. There are several ways of relating to shame, and there is, as Tomkins puts it, "a pluralism of shames."[25] Certainly, many shames are present at the heart of my grandmother's poem. Any reading must plot the relations between my grandmother as a writer and a "well-meaning white woman" and her embeddedness in a localized as well as a general, if not universal, history of colonialism. The overwhelming identification and overidentification that the poet creates with the figure of the Indigenous woman needs to be acknowledged. But equally the poem works to bring the backdrop of colonialism into the foreground. It makes us feel the relations of contact.

Certainly her vicarious shame felt on behalf of Indigenous Canadians gets written on the shamed relation between the Indigenous mother and the "half breed" daughter. But one needs to recognize that in the context of representing frontier colonialism, white shame would usually have been pushed away from public consciousness. Who knows where the impetus came from, but obviously my grandmother felt a need to speak up. Perhaps it was pride in her homeland that made her sensitive to the shame of what whites were doing to the Indigenous. She was by all accounts a proud, tough woman. She would have had to be; colonialism as a shame culture would hardly sanction lady poets to speak of interracial shame. Within the limits of this culture, the fine details become of interest. The color and texture of hair being brushed, the absence of the white father, the distance the daughter gains through education and implicitly the "white man's way," the bright houses in the suburbs, and finally the door that divides the mother from her daughter forever—these are ways in which the poet brings the shame forward. In plotting these characteristics, the shame of the poet meets and draws on someone else's shame. Nonetheless, her own shame is palpably there; and in speaking of it the poem cannot help but spread its affect and effects widely. At the very least, her poem goes against the way that ancestral shame is so often "'buried alive' . . . one can be shameless in attempting to hide it."[26]

RELATING TO RELATIVES

After a presentation I gave about my grandmother and her poem, a colleague pointed out that I not only look like my grandmother but also have the same cadences in my writing. At first I was taken aback, or rather I was interested, piqued by something akin to pride. Then in response to this, I felt abashed, if not ashamed. A visceral connection to the dead is an unnerving experience. The pride I experienced had something to do with my grandmother's having been a very striking woman, so the remark felt like a compliment that forged a bond across the generations. Also, because there is so little left of my maternal family, it made me feel close and engaged within a web of relations. She seems to stand apart from her contemporaries, who presumably would not have thought of writing about, or relating so closely to, Indigenous women. But as her granddaughter, my defense of her practices places me within the ambit of their current assessment as shameful. To feel pride in ancestral shame is a strange thing and can exacerbate that shame.

To return to my argument in chapter 2 about the habitus, I wonder if one can inherit an aptitude for feeling. Certainly in many arguments, as in Ukai's, it seems one can: "Shame can be gifted beyond generations." On one reading, ancestral shame resides in passing on the object of shame—skeletons in the family closet. In a way, this makes sense of my initial shamed reaction to my grandmother's writing of an interracial scene. Who was she to speak? That question belongs to a paradigm of criticism that cannot be applied (or at least not easily) to women of my grandmother's generation. It also misses the plurality of shame and the ways shame produces more shame, more feeling, reactions, relations, and types of relatedness.

Other relations of shame need to be explored. Could ancestral shame also refer to the manner in which we may inherit a capacity for being interested in ways that open us up to shame? Does my shame in relation to my grandmother relate to a similar structuring of shame within the familial habitus? These are tough questions that could easily slip into a pop psychology of histories. But the repetition of love lost, of compassion rearranged into another's shame, these are both echoes of the chiasmus effects of shame. The narration of shame distributes its effects all over the place. It connects people and places in strange ways. Shame creates tangled lines of relation. To flesh out an ethics of response to shame requires a hyperawareness of the way it moves and the connections it relates. This is what shame does: it makes our bodies horribly sensitive. In this, perhaps the shame my grandmother imparted to me is a gift.

Considering affect in the contact zone is to be returned inescapably to the space of copresence. It is to be related to history in the intimate way we are related to relatives, especially those who were part of historical moments of contact between whites and Indigenous peoples. White women, like my grandmother, may have related their shame in ways that heaped a twisted subjectivity onto the objects of shame. But equally, her relating of that moment is generative of my habitus and its capacity to feel shame—to be continually unsettled in my empathy. The task, as LaCapra puts it, is to earn the entitlement to write shame. As my interlocutor to the first telling of this story of ancestral shame put it, I've still got some things to learn.[27]

5

Writing Shame

I FIRST BEGAN TO HAVE SYMPATHY for Charles Darwin when I read about the terrible toll his research and writing seem to have taken on his body. Apparently he went through long bouts of illness during which he continually threw up, had diarrhea, and was forced to take to his bed. He believed in what we now call alternative therapies, especially hydrotherapy, which sometimes worked for him.

I thought about Darwin when, between waking and thinking, I felt the presence of something dreadfully pressing. Ah yes, the book. And then I retched. This kept happening as I pondered my case. There was no great stress in my life. I was on research leave far away from the pressures of my job, and all I had to do was to write, rewrite, and rewrite this book. I tried to ignore this little routine my body had set up. That didn't work; the body insisted I pay attention. I reviewed what was happening. I would go to bed and sleep soundly in a seemingly dreamless state. On waking I would notice that my hands and feet hurt. It became clear that during the night my body contorted itself: my fists tightened, my feet tensed, and I ground my teeth. I consulted a Chinese herbalist, who gave me a dreadful tasting potion and advised me that my blood pressure was extremely low. "Good for an elite athlete," she said, looking dubiously at my state of physique. A Western doctor said I was suffering from "fight or flight" syndrome and recommended I take vigorous exercise last thing at night. He also suggested a hockey mouth guard to protect some of my diminishing tooth structure. The remedy was too much to countenance, so I ground on.

I lectured my body sternly, but it wouldn't listen to reason. To my mind, it was just the pressure of a deadline that was making me ill. All I had to do was get the manuscript done before it finished me. A friend, worried about my deteriorating state of health, was unconvinced by my expedient logic. She has been researching violence, shame, and honor among young men. She quickly pointed out what I should have known and, indeed, what I have already written: shame is a painful thing to write about. It gets into your body. It gets to you.

Of course shame is a painful thing to write about: an exposure of the intimacies of selves in public. But it wasn't quite the shame of exposure I was feeling. Something else was agitating me. As I considered in chapter 1, it's possible that reading too much about affect leads to hypochondria. It certainly makes you more aware of the operation of different affects in the body. I decided from the outward signs that it wasn't exactly shame my body was exhibiting. What my doctor had termed fight or flight was closer to what Tomkins would call fear-terror. Yes, that was what I felt: the clenching of fists and jaw, the twisting and tensing of feet. It dawned on me that I was experiencing the terror of not being equal to the interest of my subject. The idea that I would not interest readers triggered what seemed to be a mixture of fear and shame.

There is a shame in being highly interested in something and unable to convey it to others, to evoke the same degree of interest in them and to convince them that it is warranted. This is heightened when the questions you want to ask seem so large they escape any one authority. My friend was, once again, helpful.[1] She reassured me that it was the time for big questions and that I wouldn't fall flat on my face. It was a kind comment; maybe I will and maybe I won't. As they say in Australia, sometimes you have to take a punt.

The punt, or the risk of writing, is always that you will fail to interest or engage readers. Your deep interest in the topic exacerbates this. Disappointment in yourself looms large when you can't quite get the words right or get the argument across. Simply put, it's the challenge of making the writing equal to the subject being written about. The gulf between the two may bring on the feeling of being a sham or, as I'll argue in this chapter, a deeper shame. Lynn Barber, a journalist who has interviewed some of the great writers of our time, describes the former. Reflecting on her interview with the prolific essayist Christopher Hitchens, Barber finds an undertow: "Perhaps his sense of imposture is the one all writers have—that they care more about writing than they do about their subject."[2]

This comment strikes a chord. Feeling like a fraud is routine in the modern university. We often teach classes in areas in which we are not trained; we take on administrative tasks for which we have no formal instruction whatsoever. By and large we muddle along, pretending we know how to do Excel spreadsheets or what a budget should look like. Feeling like a sham is the price one pays for living in a multiskilled world.

But by calling it imposture, Barber paints the problem in terms that threaten to slip from the fairly minor to the major. *Imposture* implies making it up, hiding behind a mask of competence. Etymologically *shame* comes from the Goth word *Scham,* which refers to covering the face. The crucial element that turns sham into shame is the level of interest and desire involved. There is no shame in being a sham if you don't care what others think or if you don't care what you think. But if you do, shame threatens. To care intensely about what you are writing places the body within the ambit of the shameful: sheer disappointment in the self amplifies to a painful level.

My argument in this chapter is about writing shame, a phrase I use to capture both the affective, bodily feeling of betraying interest, and also about how we might envision writing shame as part of an ethical practice. Shame forces us to reflect continually on the implications of our writing. The insights provided by different kinds of writers will show that writing shame is a visceral reminder to be true to interest, to be honest about why or how certain things are of interest. The writers I focus on are from quite different realms. They are a novelist, a witness and victim of atrocities, and a philosopher. There is, of course, a difference between the objectives of a fiction writer and those of an academic one. Crudely put, if you make things up, does it matter that you care more about your writing than your subject matter? Conversely, if you are an academic writer, why should you even care about writing rather than "ideas"? The insights of writers as different as Stephen King, Primo Levi, and Gilles Deleuze make these distinctions disappear. Exemplary in writing about shame, they discuss the need for modesty, what we can learn about writing from the body in shame, and above all they provide lessons about writing without affectation. None of them escapes the toll writing takes on the body. In the most extreme case, Levi speaks of having to write the story of Auschwitz as a "violent impulse to the point of competing with . . . elementary needs."[3] If the inclusion of Levi in the company of a popular American writer and a French philosopher is shocking, it needs to be remembered and celebrated that Levi's great passion was writing, a love he turned to as something separate from testifying. Levi was an example to all who aspire to write.

ACADEMIC ANXIETIES

Sometimes it seems that academics do not aspire to be writers. In fact the aspiration may be ridiculed in a society with a prevailing belief that academics cannot write. Even within the humanities, the notion of the researcher as writer is still, or is once again, considered dubious. Of course, whole disciplines have had their "literary turns," and "poetics" is appended to everything from ethnography to history. But the question of writing per se has tended to be brushed aside in the guise of "writing up research." While the pretense of academic writing as purely objective might be fading, there's little thought about what will replace the dominant mode of "writing up." The gulf between research and writing is becoming especially fraught with the increase in academic studies about emotions and affects. Kathleen Woodward, an American literary critic, argues that "academic emotions . . . serve as compensations for the anesthetization of the emotions in everyday life." She raises some of the problems academics face when dealing with the affective: "the stringent rules of emotionless rationality, especially in regards to research and writing."[4]

Those emotionless rules can protect the researcher from being invaded by the affective and troubling nature of research. George Devereux, an eclectic thinker, provided one of the most interesting takes on social scientific methods. In the 1960s Devereux founded an area of research called ethnopsychiatry. One of his most influential books is entitled *From Anxiety to Method in the Behavioral Sciences.*[5] Having first studied physics under the tutelage of Marie Curie, he was influenced by Mauss in his PhD in anthropology, and consequently he trained as a psychoanalyst. His work remains important in the clinical treatment of mental disorders in non-Western countries and has influenced Gilbert Herdt and Robert Stoller's anthropological work on sexuality.[6]

Devereux's ideas on how methods within social science both protect and promote anxiety in the researcher are fascinating. He argues that the singularity of the social sciences is that they deal with affective material: "the analysis of man's conception of himself." Of the three great revolutions—provoked by Copernicus, Darwin, and Freud—he remarks, "It was easier to be objective about the heavenly bodies than about man as an organism, and the latter easier than objectivity about man's personality and behavior."[7] The trouble or, conversely, the great quality of the sciences of man (in particular, anthropology, sociology, and some branches of psychology) lies in the difficulty in clearly distinguishing materials that come from outside (the subject, the field) and from inside (his or her own emotional reactions). The researcher has to struggle with these emotional reactions and anxieties. . . . The researcher is, in one way or another, the subject and object of the knowledge that he/she elaborates.[8]

Devereux puts his argument bluntly: "In short, behavioral science data arouse anxieties, which are warded off by a counter-transference inspired pseudo-methodology; this maneuver is responsible for nearly all the defects of behavioral science."[9] He argues for three points that produce the real data of behavioral science:

1. The behavior of the subject.
2. The "disturbances" produced by the existence and observational activities of the observer.
3. The behavior of the observer: His anxieties, his defensive maneuvers, his research strategies, his "decisions" (= his attribution of a meaning to his observations.[10]

Following from this Devereux includes as data his attempts to understand his own behavior, both as a field ethnologist and as a clinical psychoanalyst. He also demands that his colleagues take notes on their own affective behavior. For instance, following a film on Aboriginal circumcision rites, he asks for and receives from his colleagues written summaries of their dreams and symptomatic reactions. Of these he notes that "one of the sanest persons" he knows has written that he had no dream but on waking he was very tired and thirsty. To which Devereux responds: "Is it possible that you may have spent the night struggling against the emergence of an anxiety laden dream, or that you have had to make a tremendous effort to forget the dream you may have had?" His colleague says the explanation is "plausible."

I wonder what kind of professional atmosphere this kind

of interrogation might have promoted? It certainly might have charged departmental seminars in interesting ways. While for many it probably seemed a bit much, the constant inquiry into how people are affected by their objects of study is impressive. In seminars I attend, I am quite often amazed at how this affective level of what Devereux calls data is simply ignored as the researcher presents findings on quite shocking material. Seemingly no thought is given to how the material will affect the audience or how, indeed, it affected the researcher. Often as I sit listening to these unimpassioned accounts I think: You sat there listening to the woman telling you this? How did she feel about this recounting? How did you react? How did you sleep that night? I am all too aware that these remarks could descend into the touchy-feeling and render the exercise a solipsistic focus on the researcher. On the other hand, what hubris to think that the body's reactions to another's emotions and affects are strictly within the realm of the personal and therefore devoid of academic/scientific interest. This is the gist of Devereux's argument: the in-between space of the researcher and the researched generates a great deal of data or information. How bodies are affected gives crucial insight into the research process and the object of the study. Including them in the written presentation of the research seems to be a sensible idea.

Devereux's approach highlights that "a realistic science of mankind can only be created by men most aware of their own humanity precisely when they implement it most completely in their scientific work."[11] In his eclecticism and passion he resembles Mauss. As in Mauss's desire to found a sociology of humanity, in Devereux we hear a reminder of that passionate quest to study humanity in all its wonderful weirdness. Not for nothing does Devereux focus on the affective, bodily reactions that the researcher may have in regard to his or her object. This, he argues, is interesting and "illustrates the *range* of phenomena." He argues that his anecdotes, what he calls cases, give "an analysis of range—and, therefore, also an analysis in depth—of the scientist's reactions to his data and to his 'sciencing.'"[12] As Tobie Nathan, a psychologist and now director of the Centre de l'ethnopsychiatrie in Paris, states of the effect of Devereux's writing: he seeks to interest his reader. Addressing readers unfamiliar with Devereux, Nathan writes, "Let yourself go! . . . You will come out metamorphosed, filled with questions . . . and more human."[13]

This energy, aimed at once at producing scientific research and gaining readers' interest, is, at times, lacking even in work on emotion and affect. As Sedgwick and Frank point out, current treatises on affect tend to lack feeling.

> Affect is treated as a unitary category, with a unitary history and unitary politics. There is no theoretical room for any difference between, say, being amused, being disgusted, being ashamed, and being enraged. . . . Genres are differentiated not in relation to the kind of affect they may evoke or generate but, far more simply, by the presence or absence of some rarified substance called Affect.[14]

An abstract way of approaching affect and emotion places the writing itself in an uninterested relation to affect. This is a contradiction in terms—affects are inherently interested. For Sedgwick and Frank, a distanced and general use of affect represents "a theoretical decision as if what is presented could not finally *be* 'theory' if it made any definitional room at all for the qualitative differences among affects."[15] You can feel Devereux shudder at the methodological slackness and the waste of potential material. How can you represent a sense of emotional and affective intensity if the feeling in question is generalized in the amorphous category of Affect?

Against this drab picture of affect, there are other possibilities. For instance, the writings of Mauss, Tomkins, Devereux, and Sedgwick inspire a breadth of vision and a desire for precision. These four depart from the dogmatic assumptions of their disciplines. In different ways they ask, why and how do we do the things we do? I'm also inspired by the tiny distinctions in their scientific descriptions of human beings as affective organisms. The detail of their analyses of distinct emotions or affects is exciting.

An epistemological point hovers in the background: a precise emotion demands precise description. It is the precision of a description that allows for a larger comprehension of what affects and emotions can do. In other words, affects have specific effects; it makes no sense to talk about them outside this understanding. Precise descriptions of the affective—in my case, shame—can also affect other concepts: ideas such as the body and its relation to writing or rethinking an ethics of writing. A general gesture to Affect won't do the trick. If we want to invigorate our concepts, we need to follow through on what different affects do, at different levels. The point needs to be stressed: different affects make us feel, write, think, and act in different ways. Shame, for example, works over the body in certain ways. It does this experientially—the body feels very different in shame from how it feels in enjoyment—but it also reworks how we understand the body and its relation to other bodies or, for want of a better word, to the social. This matters at the level of theory. It matters in terms of what we want writing to do.

WORDS AND THINGS

Like many, I became an academic mainly because the relation between words and things fascinates me. Words and things: many will recall *Les mots et les choses,* the French title for Michel Foucault's book *The Order of Things*.[16] It traces how "things," produced in relationship to different orders of knowledge, have been arranged over the centuries. It is also charged with an insistence that things don't have to be the way they are. Working as a waitress in Montreal, I read Foucault's book in a bar between shifts. To say that it opened new vistas is not overly dramatic. As I read I would look up, listen, and observe people's interactions. Sometimes you can catch a whole world-view from a snippet of bar talk. The relation between words and things is not just cerebral; it is, I think, at the very heart of what makes humans interesting.

It's a strange segue from Foucault, one of the great philosophers of the twentieth century, to Stephen King, one of the most popular novelists. But they are both entranced by the relationship between words and things. King is, of course, most noted for his horror stories. He is prolific, with some thirty-nine novels to date, many of which have been made into films. Something like three million people have read each of his novels. His wide appeal may be why King's writing is disdained by many. It's that old bugbear of commercial success: how could someone that popular be any good? King's meditation *On Writing* responds to this prejudice. In the genre of memoir but also marked with the precision of an instruction manual, it's a set of instructions for writing with a gripping narrative. It makes me wonder, when narrative is the most human of needs, why it is so rarely present in theoretical writing. King's narratives are so absorbing no one thinks to ask about how they are written. In the preface to this book, King relates a conversation he had with Amy Tan, another popular writer:

> I asked Amy if there was any one question she was *never* asked during the Q-and-A that follows almost every writer's talk—that question you never get to answer when you're standing in front of a group of author-struck fans and pretending you don't put your pants on one leg at a time like everyone else. Amy paused, thinking it over carefully, and then said: "No one ever asks about the language."[17]

King reflects that the question of a writerly relation to language is asked of "the DeLillos and the Updikes and the Styrons," but he adds, "Many of us proles also care about the language, in our humble way, and care passionately about the art and craft of telling stories on paper."[18]

As a writing coach, King is great—tough and funny. He has made me think several times about each sentence I've written since I read his book. His depiction of writing and shame is instructive. In King's memory, it was a high school teacher who first made him aware that there might be something shameful about his writing. The teacher asked him why he wrote such junk: "I had no answer to give. I was ashamed. I have spent a good many years since—too many, I think—being ashamed about what I write."[19]

King finally got over the shame she induced. But he remains very clear about writing he sees as shameful: writing that lacks honesty. Honesty for him includes the precise relationship between words and things; he is also concerned with the structural aspects of writing such as grammar and dialogue. His rant about words makes poststructuralism seem pragmatic:

> The word is only a representation of meaning; even at its best, writing almost always falls short of full meaning. Given that, why in God's name would you want to make things worse by choosing a word which is only cousin to the one you really wanted to use?[20]

If King is not above shaming his readers into being good writers—"it's *writing*, damn it, not washing the car or putting on eyeliner"—it is because he is passionate about honest writing. Being honest about writing also means becoming an honest reader. King is scathing about "people who read very little (or not at all in some cases) [and then] presume to write and expect people to like what they have written." While academics read a lot, I sometimes wonder whether we read only for ideas, with a focus on what we're trying to write rather than on the writing that we're reading. King is very good at describing the effects of being read: waiting as his Ideal Reader (his wife) reads a draft, "I try to watch her when she gets to a particular scene, hoping for at least a smile or—jackpot, baby!—that big, belly laugh with the hands up, waving in the air."[21]

How that reaction warms a writer's heart. This framing of his nervous expectation explains what King means by honesty. Has he interested the reader in what he cares about so passionately? King is also up-front about the toll such interest takes: "You can approach the act of writing with nervousness, excitement, hopefulness, or even despair." He concludes, "Come to it any way but lightly." He repeats in italics: *You must not come lightly to the blank page.*[22]

King's lessons have stayed with me. His arguments are challenging. For King, the goal of writing is a telepathic connection between reader and writer, whereby the reader "catches" the writer's interest. It's what you're trying to say to the reader, not how good you sound to yourself. It's about recognizing what you're trying to *do* to the reader (although strangely enough, King doesn't talk about the effects of horror on the reader) and what writing does to the writer. Simply put, writing affects bodies. Writing takes its toll on the body that writes and the bodies that read or listen.

In another vein, Sedgwick and Frank write of the deep tiredness that overcame them while reading Tomkins's writing about affect. "I often get tired when I'm learning a lot."[23] That physical exhaustion is compounded when the material demands to be taken in, in demanding ways. My first experience of this was years ago when I was researching anorexia. At times it all just hurt. Reading research and interviews, watching tapes of clinical sessions, dredging up my own experiences as a sort of touchstone—the effort of bringing all these layers of reality together was deeply challenging, especially as a young researcher. On other projects, working through a particular knot of affect, experience, and theory has resulted in strange spatial dreams in which I am inside "the problematic." Sometimes the battle in the night results in inspiration, sometimes just in deep fatigue.

BODY-AFFECTS

Writing is a corporeal activity. We work ideas through our bodies; we write through our bodies, hoping to get into the bodies of our readers. Writing about "negative affects" such as shame or disgust provides graphic proof of what Devereux understands as the affective realm of the human sciences. We study and write about society not as an abstraction but as composed of actual bodies in proximity to other bodies. This point is elaborated by Gilles Deleuze. His ideas about bodies shake up assumptions about their boundedness—what we take to be our own and how one body relates to others. Influenced by Spinoza, he argues that the body is not a unified entity but is composed of many moving elements. Affects play a crucial role in how assemblages are composed and decomposed. As Moira Gatens has argued, affect leads us to "question commonsense notions of the privacy or 'integrity' of bodies through exposing the breaches in the borders between self and other evidenced by the contagiousness of 'collective' affects."[24] Affect in this model does not impinge on the body from the outside, nor does it erupt from the inside. Deleuze's model makes such distinctions incomprehensible. Gatens sums it up as "a body in constant interchange with its environment . . . the body as a nexus of variable interconnections, a multiplicity within a web of other multiplicities."[25]

In this model, the body is defined by kinetic and dynamic relations. It helps to picture the body as composed of thousands of bits all whizzing around. At the level of kinesis, "it is the relations of motion and rest, of speeds and slownesses between particles that define a body, the individuality of a body."[26] This recalls Massumi's point about the ways in which feelings are in motion with other feelings. Massumi finds evidence of this in scientific ideas about propriocentrism—the sensors that register the body's movements in relation to its own movement:

> *It moves as it feels and it feels itself moving.* . . . The slightest, most literal displacement convokes a qualitative difference, because as directly as it conducts itself it beckons a feeling, and feelings have a way of folding into each other, resonating together, interfering with each other, mutually intensifying, all in unquantifiable ways apt to unfold in action, often unpredictably.[27]

Interest in the body's feelings and movements goes back to William James's theory of emotions (1872), which also emphasizes the different feelings of different emotions.[28] James's theory of how we feel goes like this: (a) I perceive a lion; (b) my body trembles; (c) I am afraid. In other words, the body perceives itself perceiving the trigger of emotion, which sets off movement (trembling), and then gets named as a cognitive state (fear). Or there is Deleuze's description of this sequence: (a) the perception of a situation; (b) the modification of the body; (c) the emotion of consciousness or the mind.[29]

The other way Deleuze defines the movement of bodies is through their dynamic interactions with other bodies: "A body affects other bodies, or is affected by other bodies; it is this capacity for affecting and being affected that also defines a body in its individuality." Thinking, writing, and reading are integral to our capacities to affect and to be affected. In Deleuze's terms, this "is a complex relation of speed and slowness, in the body but also in thought, and it is a capacity for affecting and being affected, pertaining to the body or thought."[30] In everyday life we experience this abstract thought in practice. William Connolly describes the relationship between thinking, bodies, and sensibilities as "everyday techniques, both gross and subtle, by which thinking is altered in its direction, speed, intensity, or sensibility." He asks us to ponder how, say, listening to Mozart or "going dancing to music that inspires and energizes" will change the "the relays that connect word, gesture, memory, sound, rhythm, mobility, image, and thinking."[31]

SHAME AND GLORY

Deleuze's ideas about the capacity of bodies to affect and to be affected are forcefully conveyed in his discussion of T. E. Lawrence's depictions of shame and glory. Lawrence of Arabia was the heroic Englishman in the desert. He was also the writer of the *Seven Pillars of Wisdom* and *The Mint,* which recounted in part his misadventures and traumas, which included being raped.[32] The man and his writing were steeped in shame and honor.

Deleuze is particularly interested in what he calls "the subjective disposition" of Lawrence's writing. We could more simply say that Lawrence's writing was heavily autobiographical and psychological, but Deleuze shifts the meanings of those terms. He starts with an appreciation of Lawrence's skill as a portraitist, citing these descriptions:

> "Though usually merry, he had a quick vein of suffering in him"; "his mind, like a pastoral landscape, had four corners to its view: cared-for, friendly, limited, displayed"; "upon his coarse eyelashes the eyelids sagged down in tired folds, through which, from the overhead sun, a red light glittered into his eye sockets and made them look like fiery pits in which the man was slowly burning."[33]

The deftness with which Lawrence paints characters is remarkable. As Deleuze puts it, "The finest writers have singular conditions of perception that allow them to draw on or shape aesthetic percepts like veritable visions."[34] Deleuze elaborates this claim through the notion of a subjective character or disposition. This is something quite beyond a personal identity. If we remember that for Deleuze there is no unified person as such, then the idea of an autobiographical or personal style of writing becomes impossible. Rather, the subjective for Deleuze is the affective assemblage of bodies of different orders and elements. "Lawrence's writing, his style, makes use of this . . . the subjective disposition, that is to say, the force through which the images are projected is inseparably political, erotic, and artistic."[35]

In an echo of King's admonition about honesty, Deleuze also notes how true Lawrence's images are. "The images Lawrence projects into the real are not inflated images that would sin by false extension, but are valid solely through the pure intensity, whether dramatic or comic, that the writer is able to give to the event." Lawrence doesn't portray just people in this way; he applies the same intensity to abstractions and ideas—what Deleuze calls "entities." As part and parcel of Lawrence's subjective disposition, and indeed perhaps of his honesty as a writer, he has "a gift for making entities live passionately in the desert, alongside people and things, in the jerking rhythm of a camel's gait."[36]

This gift becomes pronounced in Lawrence's depiction of shame. In Deleuze's words: "Never before has shame been sung like this, in so proud and haughty a manner." It's here that the writer, the writing, an idea, and bodies all meld. Lawrence's shame is not the result of a simple psychological quality that is to be explained by some aspect of his person, such as his putative homosexuality. Deleuze makes such characterizations of Lawrence's shame beside the point. Shame is a product of the machine of subjective disposition, which produces shame as both idea and affect. The subjective, in Lawrence's case, is deeply connected to the context in which he lives and writes. Deleuze describes some of the prompts to Lawrence's shame. He was an Englishman in the desert masquerading as an Arab. "Shame is first of all the shame of betraying the Arabs, since Lawrence never stops guaranteeing English promises that he knows perfectly well will not be kept."[37] In Lawrence's words: "I must take up my mantle of fraud."[38]

In *T. E. Lawrence: An Arab View*, Suleiman Mousa gives

a historical account of Lawrence's shame. Mousa quickly
sketches early conditions that may have produced Lawrence
as shame-prone. Lawrence's father had four daughters with
his first wife before eloping with the governess, Lawrence's
mother. He not only left behind his first family, he also cut
any links by changing his name from Chapman to Lawrence.
T. E. Lawrence therefore grew up with the stigma that his
mother was from another class, his father masqueraded under
another name, and their offspring were illegitimate. According
to Mousa, Lawrence's mother was "possessed of an excessive
piety which was perhaps an act of expiation for her illicit
love."[39] Lawrence obtained a scholarship to Oxford by reason
of his Welshness, another shameful little detail. He was born
in Wales, where the family stayed only briefly, because his
father needed somewhere cheap to live after he had run away
with his mistress.

After Lawrence attended the university, his interest in
archaeology took him in 1910 to the Middle East, where he
learned Arabic. Mousa's sources say he didn't speak Arabic terribly well, although he portrays himself as capable of passing
as an Arab. Soon after his arrival he began to dress in Arab
clothing. Mousa writes of that period: "One of the secrets of
his later success was his ability to penetrate the inner self of
the Arab individual." When World War I broke out, Lawrence
found himself unhappily employed in the British Intelligence
Service. When his request to transfer to the Arab Bureau was
turned down, Lawrence resorted to intriguing tactics. Mousa
reports that he approached his goal by "capitalizing on his
superiors' mistakes, exposing their ignorance and inefficiency
and even revealing their grammatical errors and ridiculing
the style of their reports."[40] This grammatical humiliation
worked, and Lawrence was to be involved in the Arab Revolt,
which was, of course, his stepping-stone to fame.

Mousa's summation of Lawrence's character was that
he had two natures. "His 'first' nature led him to brave the

elements and to take troubles and difficulties in his stride, without fully satisfying his excessive ambition." This nature led to "his supplementary bragging, falsification and fabrication, which helped to give a picture pleasing to his imagination. . . . At the same time, his 'second' nature aroused the conscience of the educated man in him, who would act as auditor and judge." As Mousa puts it, this combination makes for an uncomfortable feeling: "Deep within himself, Lawrence knew that the greater part of his fame was based on fraud." He was driven "in the hope of atoning for earlier mistakes, which haunted him in secret."[41] In this we hear clearly the passage from sham to shame.

While Deleuze's account of Lawrence's character concurs with much of what Mousa wrote some thirty years earlier, his interests led him to consider what Lawrence's shame means for a philosophy of the body. Lawrence, writes Deleuze, "has shame because he thinks the mind, though distinct, is inseparable from the body." This has a particular meaning and implication. "The body is not even a means or a vehicle for the mind, but rather a 'molecular sludge' that adheres to all the mind's actions."[42] In this we can't forget how proud Lawrence was of his physical strength, nor can we forget that he was tortured and belatedly admitted to having been raped by the bey in 1917. Deleuze sees in Lawrence's account a particular form of shame:

> The mind depends on the body; shame would be nothing without this dependency, this attraction for the abject, this voyeurism of the body. Which means that the mind is ashamed *of* the body in a very special manner; in fact, it is ashamed *for* the body. It is as if it were saying to the body: You make me ashamed, You ought to be ashamed. . . . "A bodily weakness which made my animal self crawl away and hide until the shame was passed."[43]

This feeling of shame and its relation to the body may not be as unusual as Deleuze seems to think. In many accounts of rape or torture, the splitting off from the body is one way in which victims say they were able to endure the experience. Deleuze goes on to describe what may be happening in this splitting:

> The mind begins by coldly and curiously regarding what the body does, it is first of all a witness; then it is affected, it becomes an impassioned witness, that is, it experiences for itself affects that are not simply effects of the body, but veritable critical *entities* that hover over the body and judge it.[44]

It's a lovely description, but what are these ghostly hovering critical entities? Deleuze's argument is that emotions and affects are ideas. But they are not solely of the mind. They arise out of a violent collision of mind and body. As such they are not, properly speaking, of either; they are a particular combination of thought and body in which a distinction between the two is no longer important. "Entities rise up and act on the mind when it contemplates the body. They are acts of subjectivity." In regard to writing, this is of crucial importance: the affects "are not only the eyes of the mind, but its Powers and its Words." Thus it is in writing that they are given life: "Lawrence's style is the shock of entities." In Deleuze's reading, Lawrence's depiction of shame is expressed at the limit of the body and of language, and it makes language work differently. It produces "the great visual and sonorous images" that make Deleuze compare Lawrence with William Blake: "visions" speak of shame and beckon beyond.[45] It is a shame that, as Deleuze says, is "consubstantial with being" and reveals "an insolent beauty that shows . . . at what point 'the coming out of shame was easy,' at least for a moment."

This is an immensely powerful description of the challenge of writing shame: shame is produced out of the clashing of mind and body, resulting in new acts of subjectivity consubstantial with the words in which they are expressed. In this sense, shame cannot be simply represented as if it were a quality of the person or an aspect of the situation to be reproduced. Deleuze's idea of the subjective disposition allows us to understand something of the relationship between the writer, experience, expression, affect, and its effects. Shame cannot be conceived of as an external object that could be dispassionately described, nor is it a purely personal feeling. Shame is subjective in the strong sense of bringing into being an entity or an idea through the specific explosion of mind, body, place, and history. It must also have effects that are subjective, in that strong sense, for the writer and for the reader.

Shame is the product of many forces. It is "a singular composition, an idiosyncrasy . . . marking the unique chance that *these* entities had been retained and willed, that *this* combination had been thrown and not another." As Deleuze says, one particular combination "is named Lawrence." Lawrence as a subjective disposition that produced such a powerful expression of shame is, in Deleuze's words, a "dice throw." Deleuze remarks that "Lawrence can say with Kafka: 'It was as if the shame of it must outlive him.' Shame enlarges the man."[46] In making the man larger, shame does not necessarily make him easier to understand or more likable. From Mousa's account of Lawrence, the man was complex and probably hard to be around.

If writing shame doesn't necessarily make you a good person, why have I insisted that it may have an ethical implication in how we write? Deleuze sees in Lawrence's writing a shame that reconfigures how we think about it and about the body. In this sense, shame enlarges the man, by opening up possibilities of how we conceive of the relationship between ideas and affects, or between thinking and feeling. It also provides an argument against considering expressions of shame as merely a personal affliction. Shame—so located in bodies—becomes the entity that produces the mind as "an impassioned witness." While many have argued that shame is about self-evaluation or, more precisely, the evaluation of the self by the self, Deleuze's argument breaks with a tendency to conceptualize shame in banal psychological terms as an interior quality. Shame in Deleuze's description comes from a complex disposition, which is not unlike the version of the habitus I proposed in chapter 2: it combines the inherent and the lived experience of social structures—the biology and biography of a person. However, Deleuze goes further in radically depersonalizing shame. Shame is an affect that crosses many different orders of bodies. In this way, Lawrence is not a mere cipher for the shame of what the English were doing to the Arabs, nor is he a personification of a shameful history. Rather, Deleuze seems to be arguing that a new idea of shame was produced out of the dice throw that is Lawrence. It is a shame that is intimately connected with the character of empire at the time: haughty and proud, and deeply filled with shame.

SHAME, PROXIMITY, AND DISTANCE

Recall the phrase from Kafka that Deleuze uses to describe Lawrence: "It was as if the shame of it must outlive him." Deleuze concludes: "Shame enlarges the man."[47] As we've seen, shame arises from a collision of bodies, ideas, history, and place. But Lawrence as a writer is more than just a vehicle for a shameful moment in history: his writing of shame reworks its meaning and remakes the experience of shame into "an insolent beauty."

I now want to turn to Primo Levi, the writer who ensured that the shame of the Holocaust would outlive him. Kafka appears in one of Levi's remarks about writing contained in a recent collection of Levi's interviews. Having translated *The Trial*, Levi describes Kafka as possessing "an almost animalesque sensitivity, like snakes that know when earthquakes are coming."[48] This description captures how the affects of writing can penetrate the body of the writer and the reader. Levi's perspicacity is not surprising: he is the writer most associated with making us *feel* that shame is intrinsic to both humanity and inhumanity.

Levi the writer, like Lawrence before him, was a dice throw of history. An Italian Jew from Piedmont, he was arrested in 1943 for being involved in a partisan faction against the Fascists. He told the police that he was Jewish because he feared he would otherwise be executed as a partisan. His admission led to his deportation in 1944 to Auschwitz-Monowitz. He managed to survive the *Lager* because of what he describes as a combination of chance circumstances. Having graduated in chemistry before the war, he happened to end up in the Buna plant, which was part of Auschwitz and owned by the large chemical company IG-Farben. "And this was one of my great strokes of luck, because I said I was a chemist, without knowing that we were labourers in a chemical factory."[49] Levi also attributes his survival to having learned some German while reading chemistry. One of the major themes that emerge in interviews with Levi is the necessity of being able to communicate. Most of the Italians who were deported with Levi died soon after their arrival at Auschwitz because they could not understand the German or Polish orders.

Levi comes to us, in his own words, as a chemist who was made into a writer by Auschwitz. When he writes of shame, his writing makes shame work beyond its usual range. Levi is often read as a witness or as a documentalist, which, of course, correctly describes his two first books, *If This Is a Man* (1958) and *The Truce* (1963).[50] But he was also an extremely skilled writer who was proud of his craft and talked of it in precise ways. I want to consider first how his writing and testifying use shame to give us a map of humanity and inhumanity. Then I'll discuss his insights about writing, which constitute, I think, an undervalued resource.

In the spring of 1982, Primo Levi returned to Auschwitz as a tourist (his own term). His presence among a group of Italian students and professors as well as other camp survivors must have made it a remarkable tour. As Levi later recounts, an Italian interviewer points out the incongruity of the signs of normality in the town of Auschwitz. He says to Levi, "It seems today we'll eat in a restaurant at Auschwitz." Levi responds in that unique mixture of common sense and exquisite clarity that marks his writing:

> Yes, this is almost comical that there would be a restaurant at Auschwitz. I don't know what I'll eat. It seems to me almost profane, something absurd. On the other hand we must remember that Auschwitz was, is, a city where there are restaurants, theatres, even a nightclub probably. They have some in Poland too. There are children, schools, back then as now, alongside Auschwitz—a concept by now; Auschwitz is the *Lager*—this other Auschwitz of the living exists.[51]

The mind expands before the enormity of the scene. Levi, the man who wrote so carefully of his experiences in the camp, is back in its grip. But there, surrounded by a past that his writing makes part of our present, he calmly remarks that Auschwitz is a place where people live, and they must have restaurants, nightclubs, schools. The mundane fact of Auschwitz as a place where people live, eat, shop, and dance is still hard to countenance. Levi's Auschwitz, the place of horror, has grown into "our" Auschwitz, the source of shame that haunts our consciousness.

Levi's writing challenges any departmentalization or ownership of shame. It is not a personal capacity that is possessed by only some individuals. We must clearly acknowledge that the trauma of the camps and of the Holocaust belongs more closely to some: to the survivors and their relations, to Jewish people in general, to Gypsies, homosexuals, Communists, and intellectuals. How close we can get to Auschwitz is dependent on writers like Levi, but we do not all have equal rights to that proximity. Levi's writing makes one viscerally aware of distinctions in proximity—and getting too close can be a source of shame. To recall Ukai's distinction cited in the previous chapter, there is the shame of being human and shame as human. The former refers to an abstract idea about the shameful nature of humanity; the latter positions shame as inherent to us as human beings. Levi doesn't seem to subscribe to such hard and fast distinctions. He speaks about the gray zone, or the plurality and shades of shame. Deleuze describes this as "the shame of there being men who became Nazis; the shame of being unable, not seeing how to stop it; the shame of having compromised with it."[52]

Levi's writing continually avoids grandiose ideas. His desire for precision is played out in his descriptions of the everyday activities and aspirations of humankind. The honesty of his writing shames any attempt to make abstract remarks about shame. His modest voice warns against turning shame, the experience of the Holocaust, or any aspect of human behavior into an abstract point of theory—a specter of the shameful that haunts the writing of this book. It also recalls that, as LaCapra has put it, empathy needs to be understood as something one earns. Levi is a figure that cannot be appropriated; at the same time he doesn't license us to stand in awe before him. The pragmatic and practical tone of his comments on writing clearly demonstrates his purpose: to put descriptions—of shame, but equally of joy and hope—to work in furthering an appreciation of what humans can do, for bad or for good.

The first memoir of Levi's experiences in Auschwitz, *If This Is a Man,* was written soon after he returned to Turin after the war and was originally published in 1958; the second, *The Truce,* was published in 1963. In the introduction to a 1979 edition that includes both books, Paul Bailey states that, while it is a simplification, one can say that "*If This is a Man* is about a descent into, and *The Truce* about a flight away from, hell."[53] *The Truce* details Levi's long journey back home to Turin following his liberation from Auschwitz. Bailey calls it "almost all light." Despite this qualification, it is at the end of *The Truce* that Levi recalls a dream that he continued to have following his release. It is a nightmare of the darkest hues, which rips the reader's breath.

> It is a dream within a dream, varied in detail, one in sub-
> stance. I am sitting at a table with my family, or with friends,
> or at work, or in the green countryside; in short, in a peaceful
> relaxed environment, apparently without tension or affliction;
> yet I feel a deep and subtle anguish, the definite sensation
> of an impending threat. And in fact, as the dream proceeds,
> slowly or brutally, each time in a different way, everything
> collapses and disintegrates around me, the scenery, the walls,
> the people, while the anguish becomes more intense and more
> precise. Now everything has changed to chaos; I am alone in
> the centre of a grey and turbid nothing, and now I *know* what
> this thing means, and I also know that I have always known
> it; I am in the Lager once more, and nothing is true outside
> the Lager. All the rest was a brief pause, a deception of the
> senses, a dream; my family, nature in flower, my home. Now
> this inner dream, this dream of peace, is over, and in the outer
> dream, which continues, gelid, a well-known voice resounds:
> a single word, not imperious, but brief and subdued. It is the
> dawn command of Auschwitz, a foreign word, feared and
> expected: get up, *"Wstawach."*[54]

I have quoted the entirety of Levi's description because I want to hear again the clarity of his voice. The geography of affect that Levi creates in his description moves from out to in, and the freedom of the outside is always enfolded in the terror of the camp. The space of everyday life is drawn as a chimera: "a peaceful relaxed environment" that is haunted, even conjured into being, by terror. Contrary to Levi's description of the ways in which Auschwitz coexists with reality—it is a place where people ate and drank and worked and continue to do so—here in his dream, reality is always pushed away and torn apart by the outer dream, the reality of the *Lager*. The dream of the "present" fails before the dream of the past.

Years later, after Levi's reported suicide in April 1987, debate raged about why, or indeed whether, Levi had killed himself. The question was fueled by the circumstances of his death. He fell from his apartment staircase and to all knowledge did not leave a note. The desire to find Levi's death accidental is understandable. But it may also stem from a need to assuage our collective shame and guilt. As we know, several other survivors who went on to write of their experiences committed suicide. Jorge Semprun, a survivor of Buchenwald, attests to the high cost of writing about the experience of the camps, arguing that the writing is not cathartic for the writer but instead reconnects him or her with the horror of the camps. The Italian sociologist Diego Gambetta seems particularly adamant that Levi's death not be seen as suicide. Part of his reasoning is that "insofar as a survivor takes his life people are driven to interpret it as related to Auschwitz." Gambetta refutes this: "Levi's last moments cannot be construed as an act of delayed resignation before the inhumanity of Nazism." He also argues that Levi's death can be attributed to "an altogether different thing: the high personal cost of bearing witness to the Holocaust by writing about it."[55] But was this the case for Levi? Gambetta's conclusion is: "He never yielded. At most he snapped. On that tragic Saturday only his body was smashed." He relates that Levi had written to his friend David Mendel only months before his death that he was no longer haunted by the camp and no longer dreamed about it.

It's a strange and uncomfortable debate that seems to turn on whether it was the original experiences or the representation of them that resulted, or not, in Levi's suicide. Gambetta seems to be saying, if it is the former, then it is in some sense another victory for the Nazis. But if writers commit suicide because of their writing, surely we, the standers-by of history, are more fully implicated in their anguish and death. This understanding would charge our reading of their work. The shame in reading about the atrocities committed by humans on humans would be amplified by and combined with guilt and even disgust; readers might have to turn away. Would we turn away from Levi if this were the case? I hope not.

Marco Belpoliti, the editor who collected Levi's interviews, argues that in Levi's writing "there is a distance between the narrator and the listener; the narrator, of course, counsels his interlocutor, but there is always a certain distance between them."[56] This observation connects with the more theoretical points made by LaCapra about the necessity of not getting too close to, or overidentifying with, the writings of survivors. Was Levi helping us, his readers, in this exigency? For LaCapra, being too close leads to "acting out," an "unchecked identification," a confusion of self and other, whereby the experience of the other becomes incorporated in the self. Against this he advocates "the goal of a critically controlled dialogic exchange with the past."[57]

> The crucial role for empathetic unsettlement as an aspect of understanding . . . stylistically upsets the narrative voice and counteracts harmonizing narration or unqualified objectification yet allows for a terse interplay between critical, necessarily objectifying reconstruction and affective response to the voices of victims.[58]

The dialogic exchange is guided by the questions: "What is the other saying or doing? How do I—or we—respond to it?"[59] These reminders are important even if the metaphor of dialogue can be mindlessly abstract—I may "dialogue" with the past, but how can it "dialogue" with me? Strictly speaking, of course, it can't. However, as I described in the last chapter, shame and other affects can seem to get into our bodies, altering our understanding of our selves and our relation to the past. In Nussbaum's apt summation, emotions do not represent history, they get into it. In Deleuze's description of Lawrence's writing of shame, the body and mind react so as to reorder the subjective. Or in LaCapra's terms, "empathy should be understood in terms of an affective relation, rapport, or bond with the other recognized as other."[60] The unifying point seems to be that strong affect radically disturbs different relations of proximity: to our selves, bodies, pasts.

LaCapra also emphasizes that the experiences of others should not be allowed to serve present interests: "The meaning that is redeemed is typically that which is desired for the present, and figures in the past tend to become vehicles or mouthpieces for contemporary values." He is highly critical of representations of trauma that level out the distinctions between the past and the present, and between the representation and the reception of affect. Citing Flaubert's scathing comment about "le sublime à bon marché," LaCapra warns against the invocation of trauma that "may become somewhat routinized and threadbare insofar as it is repeatedly alluded to, in increasingly tedious, predictable terms."[61]

LISTENING TO LEVI WRITE

LaCapra's warning is quite at odds with the effect of Levi's writing. Levi himself, as I mentioned, made a distinction between what he called his autobiographical writings about the camp and his later "real" writing. Of the first, he talked about the absolute necessity to bear witness: "I came back from the camp with a narrative impulse that was pathological."[62] He describes the style of *If This Is a Man*:

> I wanted to recount what I had seen. . . . It is more effective to bear witness with restraint rather than with scorn: the scorn should be the reader's, not the author's, and it is by no means inevitable that the author's scorn will become the reader's. I wanted to provide the readers with the primary material for *their* scorn.[63]

Here the writer is not a ventriloquist for the reader but a catalyst. The rawness and indeed the embodiment of trauma, "the unhealing wound, in life and in memory, is what produces the need for the word, for clear communication."[64] Belpoliti equates this with Benjamin's description of the role of the storyteller: "'Having counsel' as offering the listener practical advice, norms for living, proverbs . . . woven into the fabric of real life, is wisdom."[65]

Levi repeats again and again the need for communication and the high price of not being understood. "A book," he says, "has to be a telephone that works."[66] This is, as we've seen, a pragmatic consideration painfully learned from his experience in the camp, where not being understood meant a quick death. It also became part of Levi's philosophy of writing as a craft. Writing is a tool or a technology that, like the telephone, has to work. When asked abstract questions about the nature of language, he replies bluntly, "I don't understand the question." And then he reiterates, "Language is what it is. It serves to communicate."[67] The memory of not being able to communicate still filled him with terror many years later, and one can understand why he has little truck with "writers who, beneath the din of their unhinged, uneven language, are hiding nothing at all."[68] As we've seen King later echo, for Levi writing meant communicating to his readers: "Part of the job of a writer is to get through to and capture, to win over . . . readers." When asked whether he suffered because of "what [he was] writing about or for the writing itself," Levi replies:

> No, not for what I'm writing about. I sometimes feel the
> inadequacy of the medium. Ineffability, it's called, and it's
> a beautiful word. Our language is human, born to describe
> things at a human level.[69]

Levi continually emphasizes the difference between the type of writing he did as a witness and his writing when, as he put it, he became a writer. But as in his other "paranoiac split" (being a chemist and being a writer), the two sides fed each other. In response to whether he would have become a writer if not for Auschwitz, Levi replies: "Without knowing 'what to

say,' without 'the content,' there is no story."[70] Having become
a writer rather than remaining a witness, he also speaks of the
shame of writing. He calls himself a "counterfeiter" in reference to stories that were not based in his experiences of the
camp. But he also defends this choice: "Was I supposed to
be a survivor for my entire life? Let's be clear, I am a survivor,
but I don't want to write only about Auschwitz."[71]

However, the worries remained: of "feeling false," of writing
"not to record facts but for pleasure or edification."[72] In another
interview he is explicit about "abstaining from embellishment,
from extras added in just to make the writing look good." More
emphatically, he states: "I don't write for myself, or if I do, I
tear it up, destroy what I've written. I think it's wrong to write
for oneself."[73] As is so often the case, Levi softens the brusque-
ness of his remark with another that contains the knife-twist of
honesty. He adds, "It doesn't harm anyone, but it feels like time
wasted." And then again, after more questions he returns to say,
"There is only one risk, of writing badly," which he qualifies as
writing that is useless. Evoking his technical job, he describes
how writing is close to manual labor: "You make a plan, at least
mentally, an outline, a design, and then you try to make a product as close as possible to the plan."

Whether in writing or in providing testimony, Levi's passion for his métier as a chemist continually informed his experience of being a writer. He was a great believer in biology as
a science and also as a force in life. Of his stories and the hope
they carried, he says: "I am built that way: I like to tell people
stories"; of his optimism: "This attitude of mine comes from
my roots and isn't thought out or deliberated: it's a constitu-
tional optimism." Such an attitude is also "a duty": it is a "dis-
service to the reader or humanity . . . to inject doses of pes-
simism."[74] Speaking of when he wrote *If This Is a Man*, he says,
"I committed an illogical transfer of my own personal happy
endings—which enriched me, by making me a writer—on to
all human tragedies."[75]

Driven by biology, reworked through biography, and fueled by his love of chemistry, Levi's writing is marked with
precision; as he puts it, writing is "a high precision work."[76]
Precision manifests itself in the "almost juridical form" of his
testimony in the first books, and it is always there in his arguments and his descriptions about the singularity of existence,
displayed perhaps most obviously in his novel *The Periodic
Table*.[77] Levi's description of his own survival and that of others is anchored in his sense of the singular and extraordinary
throw of the dice:

> All of us survivors are, by definition, exceptions, because in
> the *Lager* you were destined to die. If you did not die it was
> through some miraculous stroke of luck; you were an excep-
> tion, a singularity, not generic, totally specific.[78]

The attention to the specific actions and behavior of individuals in exceptional circumstances stems from Levi's "unre-
quited love for biology and zoology." Perhaps it's not surprising
that Levi should have been interested in the work of Konrad
Lorenz, the founder of ethology. Ethology is the study of animal
and plant behavior, or, as Deleuze defines it: "Ethology studies
the compositions of relations or capacities between different
things." Ethology foregrounds that "you do not know beforehand what good or bad you are capable of; you do not know
beforehand what a body or a mind can do, in a given encounter,
a given arrangement, a given combination."[79] This ethological
attention to how things are—to describing minute changes in
behavior—is paired with an acceptance that you cannot know
in advance what will happen. Precision over prediction: this describes Levi's writing about what humans do and how emotions
make us behave.

Levi's conception of humanity is, I think, in advance of
common notions of his time. Part of his inspiration came from
putting science to work within a philosophy of writing, dedicated to furthering a practical conception of humanity. His

task as a writer is to describe in the most precise way possible our human capacities. Listen to the way that Levi describes this: "I feel a quite specific and continual need to experience with my own senses the sheer presence of matter."[80] This attention to matter offers a powerful way of rethinking the questions: What can a body do? What can affects do?

Returning to Levi's account of surviving the Holocaust, we see that one of the striking aspects is the seeming lack of affect with which he takes us through the experiences of the camp. The scarce mention of affect or emotion suggests that being captured within the closed space of camp did not allow for that degree of reflexivity. Levi shows the suppression of emotion in a realm where people are stripped of their humanity. For instance, no mention of shame is made in his account of being inside. This becomes all the more shocking when at the beginning of *The Truce* and at the moment of their liberation, Levi writes of the shame that filled the survivors when the Russians soldiers entered the camp.

> They did not greet us, nor did they smile; they seemed oppressed not only by compassion but by a confused restraint, which sealed their lips and bound their eyes to the funereal scene.[81]

Levi goes on to describe the awareness in hindsight of the shame the inmates had felt at each turn of the camp's outrages. From the shame these inmates of the *Lager* felt at their own bodies exposed in the gaze of the other, Levi describes the different aspects of shame: what "the just man experiences at another man's crime; the feeling of guilt that such a crime should exist, that it should have been introduced irrevocably into the world of things that exist, and that his will for good should have proved too weak or null, and should not have availed in defense."[82]

Listen again to how Levi describes those eyes that will induce shame in individuals who thought they had nothing left to be ashamed of, men and women who thought they were no longer human. The soldiers bow their heads in shame, sowing the seeds of shame in the inmates. Levi shows how shame is contagious. As he recounts the near farce of his long and constantly backtracked route home to Turin, he comes upon many who are described in shame. The Ukrainian women who, through a mixture of Nazi propaganda and hardship, had nonetheless "assented" of their own "free will" to leave their homeland and work for the Germans: "In Germany they had found bread, barbed wire, hard work, German order, servitude and shame; now under the weight of their shame they were being repatriated, without joy, without hope."[83] For Levi, shame in its shades of gray is plural. The experiences of shame are also what reminds him of his humanity.

Levi speaks frequently about how the camps turned him into a writer. He also is clear about how they turned him into a Jew. As he puts it, "Before Hitler I was a middle-class Italian boy."[84] His experiences of the Holocaust made that identity impossible to maintain. After the war he integrated parts of his identity as Piedmontese with parts of Jewish tradition. One of the aspects of Jewish culture he came to value most was "the Talmudic tradition of impassioned but precise argument."[85] Of the many aspects of Levi that inspire, his way of combining passion and precision stands as a model of what we might hope for in writing. The passion that animates Levi's writing is like a slow burn. The lack of affect in his examples is also, at times, very precise—a lacuna of feeling that structures the text. He makes us feel the emptiness of that affectless state, how inhuman it is. When he turns to describing the slow return of humanity following the liberation, we see the different emotions that emerge as from a deep freeze. Levi's passion combined with precision powerfully challenges the current practice of writing about affects and emotion in a generalized and abstract way. This tendency uncouples writing from the real effects that affects such as shame produce in the world and for the world. Writing is interested; it is deeply embedded in contexts, politics, and bodies. Of course, the ways in which shame is written need to be carefully handled by the writer and the reader.

So what might a shame-induced ethics of writing entail? The specter of not interesting readers and the constant worry about adequately conveying the interest of our chosen topics should send a shiver down the spines of all writers. The blush of having failed to connect with readers should compel any writer to return to the page with renewed desire to do better—to get better—at this task of communicating that some of us take on. As Levi puts it, writing is like a telephone that works.

In Deleuze's description of writing shame, the stakes are high. The writer is more than a cipher conveying shameful moments. The body of the writer becomes the battleground where ideas and experiences collide, sometimes to produce new visions of life. This somewhat heroic description is tempered by King's prosaic argument about writing honestly. Finding the words to pitch ideas to your reader seems a long way from philosophy. But his insistence that writing is a serious activity that makes ideas and stories matter is not so different from Deleuze's insistence that ideas have to be generative. Ideas and writing about shame seek to generate new ways of thinking about how we are related to history and how we wish to live in the present. This is the legacy that Levi has bequeathed to us: the gift of shame. It is an uneasy task, this writing shame. How could it be otherwise when it involves a body grappling with interests, hoping to engage others?

Notes

INTRODUCTION

1. Quoted in Eve Kosofsky Sedgwick and Adam Frank, "Shame in the Cybernetic Fold: Reading Silvan Tomkins," in *Shame and Its Sisters: A Silvan Tomkins Reader,* ed. Eve Kosofsky Sedgwick and Adam Frank (Durham, NC: Duke University Press, 1995), 5.

2. Ibid.

3. Ibid., 4.

4. Ibid.

5. Ibid., 5.

6. *Blush* was inspired by Sedgwick and Frank's essay, and this book is one response to their challenge.

1. DOING SHAME

1. Kim Scott, *Benang: From the Heart* (South Fremantle, Western Australia: Fremantle Arts Centre Press, 1999), 31.

2. Quoted in Gerhart Piers, "Shame and Guilt: Part 1," in *Shame and Guilt: A Psychoanalytic Study,* ed. G. Piers and M. B. Singer (Springfield, IL: Charles C. Thomas, 1953), 16.

3. Most immediately for me this question is raised by Paul Gilroy in his book *Against Race: Imagining Political Culture beyond the Color Line* (Cambridge, MA: Harvard University Press, 2000). In a very different way it is also posed by Martha Nussbaum's *Women and Human Development: The Capabilities Approach* (Cambridge: Cambridge University Press, 2000), on human capacities, which she takes from Amartya Sen. In the humanities,

and especially in cultural theory, seemingly the interrogation of humanness can be posed only in oblique ways (for instance, about "the post human") because of the ongoing fear of humanism. This is beginning to change, and in the course of the book I engage with some recent and not so recent attempts to get beyond the impasse that "humanism is bad" has posed. Part of my argument is that this question is really interesting and pressing, requiring input from any number of disciplines.

4. Albert Camus, *The Myth of Sisyphus,* trans. Justin O'Brien (London: Hamish Hamilton, 1955): "imagine Sisyphus happy," 91; "describing," 70; "the ever virgin landscape" and "from their diversity," 89.

5. The Olympic Games were also called the Shame Games by many white and Indigenous critics. John Pilger's documentary did much to polarize the mood in Australia prior to the games. Given that there were many demonstrations, including an Aboriginal Tent Embassy set up in Victoria Park in Sydney, it was quite extraordinary how quickly the mood seemed to shift once the games began.

6. This is, of course, a wild generalization, which is countered in the Australian context by critics such as Anna Gibbs, who has precisely analyzed the circulation of affect within mainstream politics in "Contagious Feelings: Pauline Hanson and the Epidemiology of Affect," *Australian Humanities Review* 24 (December–February 2001), at www.lib.latrobe.edu.au/AHR/archive/Issue-December-2001/gibbs.html. At a high conceptual level, Moira Gatens and Genevieve Lloyd (in *Collective Imaginings: Spinoza, Past and Present* [London: Routledge, 1999]) provide an engaging framework for theorizing "collective imaginings." An obvious lacuna here is my lack of engagement with my colleague and friend Ghassan Hage, whose book *White Nation: Fantasies of White Supremacy in a Multicultural Society* (Sydney: Pluto Press, 1998) is one of the most provocative arguments about the enduring white fantasy of tolerance. However, he is unwilling to describe white middle Australia in anything other than dismissive terms. We also part company in terms of the positivity and potential that shame could have in white middle-class Australia.

7. Lauren Berlant, "The Subject of True Feeling: Pain, Privacy, and Politics," in *Feminist Consequences*, ed. Elisabeth Brofen and Misha Kavka (New York: Columbia University Press, 2001): "national sentimentality," 126; "the pain of intimate others," 129; "measure its effects," 132; "feeling politics," 133.

8. As Katrina Schlunke pointed out to me, we need to acknowledge that through the media we have all become skilled in reading images, especially of celebrities, for their emotional significance. Does Nicole Kidman look sad in that photo, or is she glad to be rid of Tom? That expression on Clinton's face is surely shame, or is it just a smirk at having got away with it? The accompanying story and heading will have already directed us in the right way to read emotions on famous faces. But equally there is implicit acknowledgment, especially in women's magazines, that knowing emotions is innate and needs only a little prodding.

9. See, for instance, Berlant's *The Queen of America Goes to Washington City: Essays on Sex and Citizenship* (Durham, NC: Duke University Press, 1997), where she dissects the popularity of different cultural representations in terms of their figuring of an American mode of citizenship and belonging. Also see Lauren Berlant, ed., *Intimacy* (Chicago: University of Chicago Press, 2000).

10. Berlant, "The Subject of True Feeling," 152.

11. Alison M. Jaggar, "Love and Knowledge: Emotion in Feminist Epistemology," in *Gender/Body/Knowledge: Feminist Reconstructions of Being and Knowing*, ed. Alison Jaggar and Susan Bordo (New Brunswick, NJ: Rutgers University Press, 1992), this and following quotes from 145.

12. Ibid., 154.

13. In this pairing of emotions and norms, Jaggar's argument presages Martha C. Nussbaum's *Upheavals of Thought: The Intelligence of the Emotions* (Cambridge: Cambridge University Press, 2001).

14. Jaggar, "Love and Knowledge," 159.

15. Ibid.

16. Ibid., 161.

17. Margaret Olivia Little, "Seeing and Caring: The Role of Affect in Feminist Moral Epistemology," *Hypatia* 10, no. 3 (1992): 12.

18. The possibility of building an artificial entity capable of experiencing emotion has, of course, been a staple of science fiction and science itself for some time. See Elizabeth A. Wilson's discussion of Kismet, the robot that MIT is trying to equip to have affects, in "Biologically Inspired Feminism: Response to Helen Keane and Marsha Rosengarten, 'On the Biology of Sexed Subjects,'" *Australian Feminist Studies* 17, no. 39 (2002): 283–85. Wilson, it should be mentioned, has done much to try to overcome some of the divides in feminism over "culture vs. science" and the introduction of neuroscience into feminism. See Wilson, *Neural Geographies: Feminism and the Microstructure of Cognition* (New York: Routledge, 1998).

19. Nussbaum, *Upheavals of Thought.*

20. Susan Oyama, "Essentialism, Women, and War: Protesting Too Much, Protesting Too Little," in *On Peace, War, and Gender: A Challenge to Genetic Explanations,* ed. Anne E. Hunter (New York: Feminist Press, 1991), 68.

21. Berlant, "The Subject of True Feeling," 129.

22. This paper eventually became part of the last chapter of my *Carnal Appetites: FoodSexIdentities* (New York: Routledge, 2000).

23. Jennifer Biddle, "Shame," *Australian Feminist Studies* 12, no. 26 (1997): 227–39.

24. Sedgwick and Frank, "Shame in the Cybernetic Fold," 4–5.

25. Ibid., 5.

26. Silvan S. Tomkins, "Shame-Humiliation and Contempt-Disgust," in *Shame and Its Sisters,* ed. Sedgwick and Frank, 134.

27. Ibid., 133.

28. As Tomkins puts it, "The total field in which shame is embedded in the central assembly of components of the nervous system at the moment will give quite different flavors to shame depending upon its intensity and upon the objects which appear to activate it and the objects which appear to reduce it" (ibid., 133–34).

29. In my *Outside Belongings* (New York: Routledge, 1996), I tried to get at an idea of singularity principally drawing on Deleuze and Agamben. I used the image of a soup being reduced to try to formulate the ways in which the singular is a condensation of several more general elements into a quite specific admixture—which may have rendered the discussion needlessly opaque.

30. Cited in Irving E. Alexander, "Silvan S. Tomkins: A Biographical Sketch," in *Shame and Its Sisters,* ed. Sedgwick and Frank, 251.

31. Sedgwick and Frank, "Shame in the Cybernetic Fold," 23.

32. See Fiona Probyn, "The White Father: Denial, Paternalism, and Community," *Cultural Studies Review* 9, no. 1 (May 2003): 60–76. Fiona's forthcoming book examines the "disappearance" of white fathers from Australian cultural history.

33. Alexander, "Silvan S. Tomkins," 256.

34. Paul Ekman, "About Brows: Emotional and Conversational Signals," in *Human Ethology: Claims and Limits of a New Discipline,* ed. M. von Cranach, K. Foppa, W. Lepenies, and D. Ploog (Cambridge: Cambridge University Press; and Paris: Éditions de la maison des sciences de l'homme, 1979). Ekman's article appears in an interesting collection on ethology, a subject that Gilles Deleuze ("Ethology: Spinoza and Us," in *Incorporations,* ed. Jonathan Crary and Sanford Kwinter [New York: Zone Books, 1992]) and more recently Moira Gatens ("Sex, Gender, and Sexuality: Can an Ethologist Practice Genealogy?" *Southern Journal of Philosophy* 35, supplement [1996]) engage with.

35. See also Wilson, "Biologically Inspired Feminism."

36. Tomkins, "Shame-Humiliation and Contempt-Disgust," 7–8.

37. I have tried to convey some of the looniness of behavioral and some feminist approaches to anorexia in a fictional essay, "The Taste of Power," in *Bodyjamming: Sexual Harassment, Feminism, and Public Life,* ed. Jenna Mead (Sydney: Random House, 1997). My first publications were on anorexia, and for some reason the experience of anorexia comes to me at times when I'm reading totally unconnected theories. In terms of a nuclear scene, my experience with that psychologist probably overdetermined my unfair aversion to the discipline.

38. Anthony Wilden, *System and Structure: Essays in Communication and Exchange* (London: Tavistock, 1972).

39. Sedgwick and Frank, "Shame in the Cybernetic Fold": "constant switching," 9; two important points, 8; "how things differentiate," 13.

40. Donald L. Nathanson, ed., *Knowing Feeling: Affect, Script, and Psychotherapy* (New York: Norton, 1996), 381.

41. Sedgwick and Frank, "Shame in the Cybernetic Fold," 10.

42. Nathanson, ed., *Knowing Feeling*; Andrew J. Strathern, *Body Thoughts* (Ann Arbor: University of Michigan Press, 1996).

43. Sedgwick and Frank, "Shame in the Cybernetic Fold," 11.

44. Brian Massumi, *Parables for the Virtual: Movement, Affect, Sensation* (Durham, NC: Duke University Press, 2002).

45. Nathanson, ed., *Knowing Feeling,* 382.

46. Silvan Tomkins, *Affect, Imagery, Consciousness,* vol. 2, *The Negative Affects* (New York: Springer; and London: Tavistock, 1963), 230.

47. Alexander, "Silvan S. Tomkins," 262.

48. Ibid., "the magnification," 216; final quotation, 220.

49. Silvan S. Tomkins, "Affect and the Psychology of Knowledge," in *Affect, Cognition, and Personality,* ed. Silvan Tomkins and Carroll E. Izard (London: Tavistock, 1965), 72; see also Tomkins's "Introduction to Affect Symposium, APA 1964," in the same volume.

50. Tomkins, "Shame-Humiliation and Contempt-Disgust," 136.

51. Jack M. Barbalet, *Emotion, Social Theory, and Social Structure: A Macrosociological Approach* (Cambridge: Cambridge University Press, 1998), 21.

52. Ibid., 8.

53. Dylan Evans, *Emotions: The Science of Sentiment* (New York: Oxford University Press, 2001).

54. Cited in Joseph Adamson and Hilary Clark, "Introduction: Shame, Affect, Writing," in *Scenes of Shame: Psychoanalysis, Shame, and Writing,* ed. Joseph Adamson and Hilary Clark (Albany: State University of New York Press, 1999), viii.

55. Cited in Nicholas Humphrey, *The Mind Made Flesh: Essays from the Frontiers of Psychology and Evolution* (Oxford: Oxford University Press, 2002), 103.

56. Ibid.

57. Given that *shame* in English comes from the Gothic form *Scham* (related to "being covered") and follows a grammatical structuring of "having shame," we could get carried away by such semantic wrangling.

58. Tomkins, *The Negative Affects,* 132.

59. Michael Lewis, "Self-Conscious Emotions: Embarrassment, Pride, Shame, and Guilt," in *Handbook of Emotions,* ed. Michael Lewis and Jeannette M. Haviland-Jones (New York: Guildford Press, 2000), 627.

60. Bernard Williams, *Shame and Necessity* (Berkeley: University of California Press, 1993), 220.

61. Both quotes from Sedgwick and Frank, "Shame in the Cybernetic Fold," 22.

62. Charles Darwin, *The Expression of the Emotions in Man and Animals* (London: John Murray, 1872), 281.

63. Wilson, "Biologically Inspired Feminism," 284–85.

64. Ibid., 284.

65. Arnold Leonard Epstein, *The Experience of Shame in Melanesia: An Essay in the Anthropology of Affect,* Royal Anthropological Institute of Great Britain and Ireland, Occasional Paper No. 40 (1984). See also Michelle Z. Rosaldo, "Toward an Anthropology of Self and Feeling," in *Culture Theory: Essays on Mind, Self, and Emotion,* ed. Richard A. Shweder and Robert A. LeVine (New York: Cambridge University Press, 1984), which was published in the same year as Epstein's monograph and is also a fascinating argument about shame, emotion, and affect. Rosaldo argues carefully about the need to distinguish "how notions of selves, affects, and persons are constructed in particular cultural milieu" beyond a stance of "hackneyed cultural relativism" (138). Her own perspective is that while the affect of shame may be universal, the emotion "depends on socially dictated ways of reckoning the claims of selves" (149). This leads her to argue that "it make[s] sense to see emotions not as things opposed to thought but as cognitions implicating the immediate, carnal 'me'—as thoughts embodied" (138). I have focused on Epstein's account rather than Rosaldo's, because it seems to be situated outside the terms then being debated—for example, culture, cognition, society.

66. Epstein, *The Experience of Shame in Melanesia*: "the constant and the variable," 34; "at the heart of shame," 3; "what kind of material is available" and "Direct access to others' experience," 35.

67. Ibid., 46.

68. Ibid., 13, 14.

69. Ibid., "one's own shame," 13; "giving-to-shame," 14; "you shame the opposing side," 14; "the shame-response is activated" and "shame . . . becomes a bridge," 19.

70. Ibid., "start with the vernacular terms," 46; "the human capacity for shame," 48–49.

71. Andrew J. Strathern, "Why Is Shame on the Skin?" in *The Anthropology of the Body,* ed. John Blacking, ASA Monograph 15 (London: Academic Press, 1977), 103.

72. Ibid., 106.

73. Ibid.

74. Ibid., 104.

75. Epstein, *The Experience of Shame in Melanesia,* 27.

76. Karen Sykes, "The Gift of Shame: The Invention of Postcolonial Society," *Social Analysis* 46, no. 1 (2002): 14, 17.

77. Ibid., 20.

78. Ibid., 23fn.

79. Ibid., 22.

80. Epstein, *The Experience of Shame in Melanesia,* 49.

81. William Connolly, *Neuropolitics: Thinking, Culture, Speed* (Minneapolis: University of Minneapolis Press, 2002), 2.

2. SHAME, BODIES, PLACES

1. Jane Harkins, "Shame and Shyness in the Aboriginal Classroom: A Case for 'Practical' Semantics," *Australian Journal of Linguistics* 10 (1990): 299. My thanks to Jane Warren for sending me this reference. Several anthropologists have raised the question of shame in Aboriginal contexts and languages (for instance, Fred R. Myers, *Pintupi Country, Pintupi Self: Sentiment, Place, and Politics among Western Desert Aboriginals* [Canberra: Australian Institute of Aboriginal Studies; and Washington, DC: Smithsonian Institution Press, 1984]). I am not suggesting that my shame has anything but a superficial resemblance to this Aboriginal concept, and of course the fear of white society that is also at play in shame is a political result of historical practices. Harkins's article is interesting because she seems motivated to apply her academic specialty to the education system, where Aboriginal children find it extremely hard to navigate cultural differences.

2. Walter Benjamin, *Illuminations,* trans. Harry Zohn (London: Fontana Press, 1992), 125.

3. Ruth Barcan's work is an exception: *Nudity: A Cultural Anatomy* (London: Berg Publishers, 2004).

4. Massumi, *Parables for the Virtual,* 18.

5. www.geollab.jmu.edu/fichter/IgnRx/Introigrx.html (accessed 12/9/02).

6. As cited on www.deh.gov.au/parks/uluru/management.html (accessed 12/9/02).

7. My thanks to Robyn and Jack Durack for taking me on a wonderful voyage and introducing me to new land and ideas.

8. Midnight Oil, "Beds Are Burning," *Diesel and Dust,* compact disc, CBS Inc., USA, 1987.

9. There is also another shame that writers rarely speak about because it is so painful: the shame of being more interested in the writing than in its putative object. I follow up on this in chapter 5.

10. Lewis, "Self-Conscious Emotions," 624.

11. Cited ibid.

12. Ibid., 628.

13. Nussbaum, *Upheavals of Thought.*

14. Graham Little, *The Public Emotions: From Mourning to Hope* (Sydney: ABC Books, 1999).

15. Katherine Young, "The Memory of the Flesh: The Family Body in Somatic Psychology," *Body and Society* 8, no. 3 (2002): 25, 47.

16. Pierre Bourdieu, "Fieldwork in Philosophy," in his *Choses dites* (Paris: Minuit, 1987), 24; my translation.

17. Ibid., 25.

18. Pierre Bourdieu, *The Logic of Practice,* trans. Richard Nice (1980; Cambridge: Polity Press, 1990), 52.

19. Ibid., "a metaphor of the world of objects," 76; "the active presence of the whole past," 56.

20. Ibid., 57.

21. Ibid., 292fn.

22. Ibid., 65.

23. Ibid.

24. Ibid., 293fn.

25. Ibid., 72; my emphasis in the last quotation.

26. Ibid., 68–69.

27. Bourdieu distinguishes between cultural capital, which is the "incorporation" (the making body) of objective markers of social distinction, and symbolic capital, which is the "world-making and changing" ability that he states is the possession of artists and writers. See Pierre Bourdieu, "Forms of Capital," in *Handbook of Theory and Research for the Sociology of Education,* ed. John G. Richardson (1984; New York: Greenwood Press, 1986), 241–58. See also Ghassan Hage, *White Nation: Fantasies of White Supremacy in a Multicultural Society* (Sydney: Pluto Press, 1998), for an interesting application of Bourdieu's ideas.

28. Bourdieu, *Logic of Practice,* 69.

29. As in Massumi's argument, affect is "irreducibly bodily and autonomic" as distinguished from emotion, which is "subjective content, the sociolinguistic fixing of a quality of experience" (Massumi, *Parables for the Virtual,* 28).

30. Bourdieu, *Logic of Practice,* 73.

31. My thanks to Marcel Fournier for these comments. For the most complete positioning of Mauss's work, see Fournier's *Marcel Mauss* (Paris: Fayard, 1994).

32. Wendy James, "'One of Us': Marcel Mauss and 'English' Anthropology," in *Marcel Mauss: A Centenary Tribute,* ed. Wendy James and N. J. Allen (New York: Berghahn Books, 1998), 20.

33. Ibid., 15.

34. Nathan Schlanger, "The Maussian Shift: A Second Foundation for Sociology in France," in *Marcel Mauss,* ed. James and Allen, 193.

35. Bruno Karsenti, "The Maussian Shift," in *Marcel Mauss,* ed. James and Allen, 76.

36. Marcel Mauss, *The Gift: The Form and Reason for Exchange in Archaic Societies,* trans. W. D. Halls (1954; London: Routledge, 1990), 80.

37. Schlanger, "The Maussian Shift," 198–99.

38. Marcel Mauss, *Sociology and Psychology,* trans. Ben Brewster (London: Routledge and Kegan Paul, 1979), 99.

39. Ibid., 98.

40. Cited in Schlanger, "The Maussian Shift," 209fn. Mauss's

experience of World War II was perhaps even more traumatic than this account suggests about his World War I experience, although by then he was writing much less. W. S. F. Pickering, "Mauss' Jewish background: A Biographical Essay," in *Marcel Mauss,* ed. James and Allen, remarks that Mauss, who did not hide the Jewishness clearly marked in his second name, Israël, may have stepped down in 1940 from his position of director of École pratique des hautes études (5th section) because of Nazi pressures.

41. Mauss, *Sociology and Psychology,* 14.

42. Ibid., 16.

43. Karsenti, "The Maussian Shift": "not a causal relationship," 76; "truly internal," 77.

44. Mauss, *Sociology and Psychology,* 10.

45. Ibid., "suggestive power of the collectivity," 10; "social grand facts," 12.

46. Michèle Barrett, "Sociology and the Metaphorical Tiger," in *Without Guarantees: In Honour of Stuart Hall,* ed. Paul Gilroy, Lawrence Grossberg, and Angela McRobbie (London: Verso, 2000), 19.

47. Norman K. Denzin, *On Understanding Emotion* (San Francisco: Jossey-Bass, 1984), 25.

48. Ibid., 22.

49. Terry Lovell, "Thinking Feminism with and against Bourdieu," *Feminist Theory* 1, no. 1 (2000): 15.

50. Lila Abu-Lughod and Catherine A. Lutz, " Introduction: Emotion, Discourse, and the Politics of Everyday Life," in *Language and the Politics of Emotion,* ed. Catherine A. Lutz and Lila Abu-Lughod (Cambridge: Cambridge University Press, 1990): "ways of thinking," 12; "serves as an operator," 10; "form of social action" and "psychobiological processes," 2.

51. Rita Felski, *Doing Time: Feminist Theory and Postmodern Culture* (New York: New York University Press, 2000).

52. Beverley Skeggs, *Formations of Class and Gender: Becoming Respectable* (London: Sage, 1997).

53. Paul Redding, *The Logic of Affect* (Melbourne: Melbourne University Press, 1999).

54. Sedgwick and Frank, "Shame in the Cybernetic Fold," 22.

55. Ibid., 20.

56. Paul Gilroy, *Against Race: Imagining Political Culture beyond the Color Line* (Cambridge, MA: Harvard University Press, 2000), 17.

57. Nathanson, ed., *Knowing Feeling,* 16.

58. Bessle Van der Kolk, "The Body Keeps the Score: Memory and the Evolving Psychobiology of Post Traumatic Stress" (1994), 8. See www.trauma-pages.com/vanderk4.htm (accessed 7/23/02).

59. Nathanson, ed., *Knowing Feeling,* 12.

60. Michael Franz Basch, "Affect and Defense," in *Knowing Feeling,* ed. Nathanson, 13.

61. Kim Mahood, *Craft for a Dry Lake* (Sydney: Anchor and Random House, 2000).

62. Ibid., 35.

63. Ibid., "a set of visceral alignments," 174; "He described it as . . . ," 224; apologizing to the dog, 194.

64. Aboriginal law dictates separation between women's and men's spiritual roles and duties.

65. Mahood, *Craft for a Dry Lake,* 124.

66. Ibid., 125. From the perspective of an anthropologist, Jennifer Biddle ("Shame," *Australian Feminist Studies* 12, no. 26 [1997]: 227–39) describes—in an embodied and therefore groundbreaking approach—other aspects of these forms of relation.

67. Mahood, *Craft for a Dry Lake,* 195.

68. Ibid., all quotations, 195; except for the phrase "scratches on the land," which is from Mary Louise Pratt's book *Imperial Eyes,* to be discussed in more detail in chapter 4.

69. Massumi, *Parables for the Virtual,* 25.

3. THE SHAMER AND THE SHAMED

1. With thanks to Dimitris Papadopoulos for this insight.

2. Wendy Brown, *States of Inquiry: Power and Freedom in Late Modernity* (Princeton: Princeton University Press, 1995).

3. Ibid., 47.

4. Benjamin, *Illuminations,* 125.

5. Zajonc cited in Stanley Rachman, "The Primacy of Affect: Some Theoretical Implications," *Behaviour Research and Therapy* 19 (1981): 279.

6. Ibid., "search for cognitive explanations," 286; "Affect is pre-cognitive," 287; "direct access," 289.

7. I am still amazed at how calling a debate emotional tends to be seen as a criticism. For instance, in the column I write for the national newspaper, the *Australian,* I raised "the emotional tone of the white boys" who guard white-Aboriginal history. Several e-mails either commented on this in an appreciative fashion, or interpreted it as an attack on men because I had called them emotional and therefore irrational, or attacked me for having been emotional in other columns and therefore "calling the kettle black." This framing of emotion as bad or as irrational is a real hindrance to furthering public debate.

8. www.backlash.com (accessed 9/26/02).

9. This and the following quote are taken from www.abc.net.au/catalyst/stories/s680863.htm (accessed 9/26/02).

10. Lutz and Abu-Lughod, eds., *Language and the Politics of Emotion,* 70, 87.

11. Ullalina Lehtinen, "How Does One Know What Shame Is?" *Hypatia* 13, no. 1 (1998): 56.

12. Resnais's film was made in 1959. Written by Marguerite Duras, it tells of the shame mixed with longing of a French woman who had a German lover during World War II.

13. Lehtinen, "How Does One Know What Shame Is?" 57.

14. Ibid., "experiences of subordination," 68; "a pervasive affective attunement," 61. See also Sandra Bartky, *Femininity and Domination: Studies in the Phenomenology of Oppression* (New York: Routledge, 1990).

15. For one such analysis, see Beverley Skeggs, *Class, Self, and Culture* (London: Routledge, 2003).

16. Tomkins, "Shame-Humiliation and Contempt-Disgust," 180.

17. Ibid., 188.

18. Sedgwick and Frank, "Shame in the Cybernetic Fold," 5.

19. Lehtinen, "How Does One Know What Shame Is?" 62, 61.

20. Ibid., 63.

21. Ibid., 72–73.

22. Elsewhere I have written against this tendency, to replace

shame with pride, which I argue can suffocate other attempts to come up with new politics. See Probyn, *Carnal Appetites*.

23. Sally Munt, "Shame/Pride Dichotomies in *Queer as Folk*," *Textual Practice* 14, no. 3 (2000): 534.

24. Ibid., 536.

25. Ibid., 538.

26. John Braithwaite, *Crime, Shame, and Reintegration* (Cambridge: Cambridge University Press, 1989), 70.

27. Ibid., 76.

28. John Braithwaite, "Shame and Criminal Justice," *Canadian Journal of Criminology* 42, no. 3 (2000): 281.

29. Ibid., 287–88.

30. John McDonald and David Moore, "Community Conferencing as a Special Case of Conflict Transformation," in *Restorative Justice and Civil Society,* ed. Heather Strang and John Braithwaite (Cambridge: Cambridge University Press, 2001), 132.

31. Ibid., 133.

32. Ibid., 138.

33. Ibid., 134.

34. Braithwaite, *Crime, Shame, and Reintegration,* 55, 72.

35. Ibid., 93.

36. Toni Massaro, "Shame, Culture, and American Criminal Law," *Michigan Law Review* 89, no. 7 (1991): 1880–944.

37. Harry Blagg, "A Just Measure of Shame? Aboriginal Youth and Community Conferencing in Australia," *British Journal of Criminology* 37, no. 4 (1997): 487.

38. Ibid., 488.

39. This is not to say that Maori have not also been the objects of white degradation, but their historical operation in relation to whites through the mediation of treaties may provide some slim grounds for respect that are completely lacking in the Australian context.

40. Braithwaite, *Crime, Shame, and Reintegration,* 162.

41. Ibid., 157.

42. Ibid., both quotations, 186.

43. Ibid., 72.

44. There have, of course, been many efforts, both theoretical and practical, in rethinking the past, present, and future

of Australia. Many of these are ongoing. Aboriginal scholars have
been instrumental in forging new relations and conceptions of the
past and present. See, for example, Jackie Huggins, "Black Women
and Women's Liberation," in *A Reader in Feminist Knowledge,* ed.
Sneja Gunew (London: Routledge, 1991); Marcia Langton, "Estate
of the Mind," in *Indigenous People's Rights in Australia, Canada,
and New Zealand,* ed. P. Havemann (Auckland: Oxford University
Press, 1999); and Aileen Moreton-Robinson, *Talkin' Up to the White
Woman: Indigenous Women and Feminism* (St. Lucia, Queensland:
University of Queensland Press, 2000). Non-Indigenous scholars
from a range of disciplines have also hugely contributed to the de-
bate. See, for instance, Heather Goodall, *Invasion to Embassy: Land
in Aboriginal Politics in New South Wales, 1770–1972* (Sydney: Allen
& Unwin, in association with Black Books, 1996); Duncan Ivison,
Paul Patton, and Will Sanders, eds., *Political Theory and the Rights of
Indigenous Peoples* (Cambridge: Cambridge University Press, 2000);
Bain Attwood, ed., *In the Age of Mabo: History, Aborigines, and
Australia* (Sydney: Allen & Unwin, 1996); and Diane Evelyn Smith
and Julie Finlayson, eds., *Fighting Over Country: Anthropological
Perspectives* (Canberra: Centre for Aboriginal Economic Policy
Research, 1997). In terms of bringing history to the present, the
collaboration of Marcia Langton and Henry Reynolds on the ABC
television series *Frontier* was crucial. In terms of responding to the
present at a conceptual level, Australian philosophers have endeav-
ored to rework the reach of certain concepts. See, for instance, Paul
Patton's use of Deleuze as a way of offering new lines of thinking in
regard to the ramifications of the *Mabo* and *Wik* decisions, in Paul
Patton, "Justice and Difference: The Mabo Case," in *Transformations
in Australian Society,* ed. Paul Patton and Diane Austin-Broos
(Sydney: University of Sydney, Research Institute for Humanities
and Social Sciences Publications, 1997). In regard to *Mabo* see
also Desmond Manderson, "Guilt, Shame, and Reconciliation,"
Quadrant 41, nos. 7–8 (1997): 96–99. Raymond Gaita's two-part
essay on *Mabo,* "Mabo Part One," *Quadrant* (September 1993):
36–39, and "Mabo Part Two," *Quadrant* (October 1993): 44–48,
raised, as did Martin Krygier's later book *Between Hope and Fear:
Hybrid Thoughts on Public Values* (Sydney: ABC Books, 1997), the

point that "where it is possible to be proud it is also possible to be ashamed" (Gaita, "Mabo Part Two," 47).

The American anthropologist Elizabeth Povinelli's "The State of Shame: Australian Multiculturalism and the Crisis of Indigenous Citizenship," *Critical Inquiry* 24 (1998): 575–610, provides an interesting argument about what she sees as the court-inspired shame that allows "the law to perform the adjustments necessary to recuperate its authority and values in a 'postideological' (post)colonial moment." Along the lines of Berlant's argument, which I discussed in chapter 1, Povinelli argues that "shame displaces issues and evidences of power, hegemony and contradiction" ("The State of Shame," 597). In response to her argument, John Frow and Meaghan Morris argue that she may have overemphasized the role of the state as monolithic and therefore missed much of the "fury of 'normal' politics that have accompanied the legal changes and challenges of the last several years" (Frow and Morris, "Two Laws: Response to Elizabeth Povinelli," in *Intimacy,* ed. Lauren Berlant [Chicago: University of Chicago Press, 1998], 425). While I find Povinelli's argument very interesting, I tend to agree that some of the abstraction with which she discusses many of the key terms, including *shame,* detract from the objective of her essay—to raise the contradictions between the state and its inclination to shame and the lived conditions of Indigenous identity. In her new project on love and carnality, Povinelli explicitly addresses how indigenous bodies are affected by the living conditions in the far north of Australia. E. Povinelli, talk presented in the Department of Anthropology, University of Sydney, August 26, 2004.

In terms of grassroots movements, the recently formed group Australians for Native Title is instrumental in bringing national and international attention to land rights.

45. Pauline Hanson, the flamboyant leader of One Nation, has had a checkered career. Expelled from the Liberal Party for her racist comments during the 1996 election campaign, Hanson went on to win the federal seat of Ipswich in Queensland as an independent MP. The One Nation Party has undergone a number of court trials concerning the legality of its status as a political party and

its right to claim electoral funding from the Queensland Electoral Commission. In 2002, Hanson stepped down as leader of the party while she defended charges of electoral fraud, of which she and One Nation cofounder, David Ettridge, were convicted in August 2003. Both were sentenced to three years in jail. For a gripping account of Hanson's rise to public prominence, see Margot Kingston, *Off the Rails: The Pauline Hanson Trip* (Sydney: Allen & Unwin, 1999). For an analysis of Hanson's affective appeal, see Gibbs, "Contagious Feelings: Pauline Hanson and the Epidemiology of Affect."

46. National Inquiry into the Separation of Aboriginal and Torres Strait Islander Children from Their Families, *Bringing Them Home: The Report of the National Inquiry into the Separation of Aboriginal and Torres Strait Islander Children from Their Families* (Canberra: Human Rights and Equal Opportunity Commission, Commonwealth of Australia, 1997).

47. For reactions to the report, see, for instance, Brigitta Olubas and Lisa Greenwell, "Re-membering and Taking Up an Ethics of Listening: A Response to Loss and the Maternal in 'the Stolen Children,'" *Australian Humanities Review* 15 (October–November 1999), at http://www.lib.latrobe.edu.au/AHR/archive/Issue-July-1999/olubas.html; and Robert Manne, "Blind to Truth, and Blind to History," *Sydney Morning Herald,* December 16, 2002, 13.

48. "Poppy Ashamed of Being Australian," *Courier Mail,* Queensland, June 28, 1997, 2.

49. *Sun-Herald,* June 8, 1997.

50. Ibid.

51. Bob Ellis, "Why We Must Hang Our Heads," *Sydney Morning Herald,* May 30, 1997, 21.

52. Sean Beresford, "A Matter Which Stirs Deep Emotion," *Sydney Morning Herald,* June 6, 1997, 14.

53. Eve Kosofsky Sedgwick, *Tendencies* (Durham, NC: Duke University Press, 1993), 25.

54. Phil Noyce cited in Sue Williams, "Home Truth," *Sun-Herald,* February 3, 2002, 1.

55. Phil Noyce quoted in Kevin Maher, "Review: Screen: Walkabout to Freedom," *Observer,* London, October 27, 2002, 9.

56. Sedgwick, *Tendencies,* 25.

57. Chris Cunneen, "Reparations and Restorative Justice: Responding to the Gross Violations of Human Rights," in *Restorative Justice and Civil Society,* ed. Strang and Braithwaite, 92. See also Chris Cunneen and Terry Libesman, "Postcolonial Trauma: The Contemporary Removal of Indigenous Children and Young People from Their Families in Australia," *Australian Journal of Social Issues* 35, no. 2 (2000): 99–116.

58. Diane Bell cited Moreton-Robinson, *Talkin' Up to the White Woman,* 122.

59. Diane Bell and Topsy Napurrula Nelson, "Speaking about Rape Is Everyone's Business," *Women's Studies International Forum* 12, no. 4 (1989): 404. The article in question was written by Bell and an Aboriginal woman, Topsy Napurrula. For an incisive account of the debate that followed, see Moreton-Robinson, *Talkin' Up to the White Woman.*

60. Huggins, "Black Women and Women's Liberation."

61. Moreton-Robinson, *Talkin' Up to the White Woman,* 145.

62. Ibid., 90.

63. Ibid., 145.

64. Paula Gunn Allen, "Some Like Indians Endure," in *Classics in Lesbian Studies,* ed. Esther R. Rothblum (New York: Harrington Park Press, 1988).

65. Moreton-Robinson, *Talkin' Up to the White Woman,* 185.

66. Sedgwick, *Tendencies,* 51.

4. ANCESTRAL SHAME

1. Cited in Satochi Ukai, "The Future of an Affect: The Historicity of Shame," *Traces* 1 (2001): 28.

2. William Yang, *Sadness,* performed in the Sydney Festival, January 20–25, 2003.

3. Ibid.

4. Ibid.

5. Édouard Glissant, *The Poetics of Relation,* trans. Betsy Wing (Ann Arbor: University of Michigan Press, 1997), 18.

6. Ibid., both quotations, 11.

7. Ibid., 8.

8. Gershen Kaufman, *Shame: The Power of Caring,* 3rd ed. (Rochester: Schenkman Books, 1992), 241, 238.

9. Cited in Bruce Robbins, "Actually Existing Cosmopolitics," in *Cosmopolitics: Thinking and Feeling beyond the Nation,* ed. Pheng Cheah and Bruce Robbins (Minneapolis: University of Minnesota Press, 1998), 1.

10. Cited in John Kraniauskas, "Translation and the Work of Transculturation," *Traces* 1 (2001): 97.

11. Mary Louise Pratt, *Imperial Eyes: Travel Writing and Transculturation* (London: Routledge, 1992), 7.

12. Ibid.

13. Clifford Geertz, *The Interpretation of Cultures* (New York: Basic Books, 1973), 30.

14. Ukai, "The Future of an Affect," 28. See also Nicolas Abraham and Maria Torok, *The Shell and the Kernel,* vol. 1, trans. Nicholas T. Rand (Chicago: University of Chicago Press, 1994).

15. Nussbaum, *Upheavals of Thought*: "the particular depth and the potentially terrifying character," 16; "intentional object," 24; "emotions always involve thought," 23.

16. Ibid., "childhood emotions," 14; "a primitive shame," 197.

17. Zoë Wicomb, "Shame and Identity: The Case of the Coloured in South Africa," in *Writing South Africa: Literature, Apartheid, and Democracy,* 1970–1995, ed. Derek Attridge and Rosemary Jolly (Cambridge: Cambridge University Press, 1998), 92.

18. Michèle Le Doeuff, "Pierre Roussel's Chiasmus," *Ideology & Consciousness* 9 (1981–82): 45.

19. Wicomb, "Shame and Identity," 97.

20. Ibid., 104–5.

21. Dominick LaCapra, *Writing History, Writing Trauma* (Baltimore: Johns Hopkins University Press, 2001), 212.

22. Ibid., 109.

23. Ibid., xi.

24. bell hooks, *Black Looks: Race and Representation* (Boston: South End Press, 1992), 25.

25. Tomkins, "Shame-Humiliation and Contempt-Disgust," 150.

26. Ukai, "The Future of an Affect," 28.

27. With thanks to Wendy Brady.

5. WRITING SHAME

1. My thanks to Jeannie Martin for her encouragement and ideas. Martin has presented fascinating research on how young men, mainly of Lebanese background, negotiate notions of honor and shame in Australia. Martin, "Shame and Violence," presented at "Synthetics," CSAA annual conference, University of Western Sydney, 2000.

2. Lynn Barber, "Life: Look Who's Talking," *Sunday Observer,* April 14, 2002, 10.

3. Cited in Carlo Ginzburg, "Just One Witness," in *Probing the Limits of Representation: Nazism and the "Final Solution,"* ed. Saul Friedlander (Cambridge, MA: Harvard University Press, 1992), 96.

4. Kathleen Woodward, "Global Cooling and Academic Warming: Long-Term Shifts in Emotional Weather," *American Literary History* 8, no. 4 (1996): 760.

5. George Devereux, *From Anxiety to Method in the Behavioral Sciences* (The Hague: Mouton, 1967).

6. Alain Giami, "Counter Transference in Social Research: Beyond George Devereux," *Papers in Social Science Research Methods—Qualitative Series,* no. 7, ed. M. W. Bauer, London School of Economics, Methodology Institute, www.ethnopsychiatrie.net/ giami.htm (accessed 7/23/2002).

7. Devereux, *From Anxiety to Method,* 3.

8. Cited in Giami, "Counter Transference in Social Research."

9. Devereux, *From Anxiety to Method,* xvii.

10. Ibid., xix.

11. Ibid., xx.

12. Ibid.

13. Tobie Nathan, "Devereux, un hébreu anarchist," www .ethnopsychiatrie/net/actu/hebranarchiste.htm (accessed 7/23/2002); my translation.

14. Sedgwick and Frank, "Shame in the Cybernetic Fold," 17.

15. Ibid.

16. Michel Foucault, *The Order of Things: An Archaeology of the Human Sciences* (New York: Vintage, 1973).

17. Stephen King, *On Writing: A Memoir of the Craft* (London: Hodder & Stoughton, 2000), x.

18. Ibid., xi.

19. Ibid., 46.

20. Ibid., 130.

21. Ibid., "it's *writing*," 117; "people who read very little," 167; "I try to watch her," 262.

22. Ibid., 118.

23. Sedgwick and Frank, "Shame in the Cybernetic Fold," 2.

24. Moira Gatens, "Privacy and the Body: The Publicity of Affect," *ASCA Yearbook,* The Netherlands (2000): 14.

25. Ibid., 7.

26. Deleuze, "Ethology," 625.

27. Massumi, *Parables for the Virtual,* 1; emphasis added.

28. For an extended discussion of James's theory of emotion, see Paul Redding, *The Logic of Affect* (Melbourne: Melbourne University Press, 1999); and Jack M. Barbalet, *Emotion, Social Theory, and Social Structure: A Macrosociological Approach* (Cambridge: Cambridge University Press, 1998).

29. Gilles Deleuze, *Essays Critical and Clinical,* trans. Daniel W. Smith and Michael A. Greco (Minneapolis: University of Minnesota Press, 1997), 123.

30. Deleuze, "Ethology": "A body affects other bodies," 625; "a complex relation of speed and slowness," 626.

31. Connolly, *Neuropolitics*: "everyday techniques," 100; "going dancing to music," 100–102.

32. T. E. Lawrence, *Seven Pillars of Wisdom: A Triumph* (1926; Harmondsworth: Penguin in association with J. Cape, 1964); and T. E. Lawrence, *The Mint* (1955; Harmondsworth: Penguin, 1978).

33. Lawrence cited in Deleuze, *Essays Critical and Clinical,* 116.

34. Ibid.

35. Ibid., 118.

36. Ibid., both quotes from 119.

37. Ibid., both quotes from 120.

38. Cited ibid., 121.

39. Suleiman Mousa, *T. E. Lawrence: An Arab View,* trans. Albert Butros (Oxford: Oxford University Press, 1966), 2.

40. Ibid., "One of the secrets of his later success," 5; "capitalizing on his superiors' mistakes," 28.

41. Ibid., all quotes from 278.

42. Deleuze, *Essays Critical and Clinical,* 123.

43. Ibid.

44. Ibid., 124.

45. Ibid., all preceding quotes from 124; following quote from 125.

46. Ibid., "a singular composition," 120; all other quotes, 121.

47. Ibid.

48. Primo Levi, *The Voice of Memory: Interviews, 1961–1987,* ed. Marco Belpoliti and Robert Gordon (Cambridge: Polity Press, 2001), 159.

49. Ibid., 212.

50. Primo Levi, *"If This Is a Man" and "The Truce,"* trans. Stuart Woolf (London: Abacus, 1979).

51. This quotation comes from a television interview conducted by Daniel Toaff and Emanuele Ascarelli, which was carried out in the journey to Auschwitz in 1982 and later broadcast on Italian TV (1/25/2001). A different translation of the same interview is published in Levi, *Voice of Memory,* under the title "Return to Auschwitz." The only real difference between the two is that, in the book, Levi is translated as saying, "I don't know if I will eat" (213), which is rather different from "I don't know what I'll eat."

52. Deleuze cited in Ukai, "The Future of an Affect," 23.

53. Paul Bailey, "Introduction," in Primo Levi, *"If This Is a Man" and "The Truce,"* 7.

54. Levi, *"If This Is a Man" and "The Truce,"* 380.

55. See www.polisci.mit.edu/BR24.3/gambetta.html (accessed 1/25/2001).

56. Marco Belpoliti, "I Am a Centaur," in Primo Levi, *Voice of Memory,* xix.

57. Dominick LaCapra, *History and Reading: Tocqueville, Foucault, French Studies* (Melbourne: Melbourne University Press, 2000), 67.

58. LaCapra, *Writing History, Writing Trauma,* 110.

59. LaCapra, *History and Reading,* 67.

60. LaCapra, *Writing History, Writing Trauma,* 212.

61. Ibid., "The meaning that is redeemed," 53; "may become somewhat routinized," 43.

62. Levi, *Voice of Memory,* 129.

63. Ibid., 251.

64. Levi cited in Belpoliti, "I Am a Centaur," xx.

65. Ibid., xviii.

66. Levi cited ibid., xix.

67. Levi, *Voice of Memory,* 86.

68. Ibid., 125.

69. Ibid., "hiding nothing at all" and "Part of the job of a writer," 125; "to describe things at a human level," 173.

70. Levi cited in Belpoliti, "I Am a Centaur," xxi.

71. Levi, *Voice of Memory,* 94.

72. Ibid., 133.

73. Ibid., this and following quotes, 172.

74. Ibid., 130.

75. Ibid., 157.

76. Ibid., 168.

77. Primo Levi, *The Periodic Table,* trans. Raymond Rosenthal (1975; New York: Schocken Books, 1984).

78. Levi, *Voice of Memory,* 122.

79. Deleuze, "Ethology," 628.

80. Levi, *Voice of Memory,* 142.

81. Levi, *If This Is a Man,* 188.

82. Ibid.

83. Ibid., 293.

84. Ibid., 262.

85. Ibid.

Index

abandonment, 3
ABC, 80
Aboriginal Reconciliation Council, 95
Aboriginal Tent Embassy, Sydney, 164n
Aborigines: being-in-country, 67; concept of shame, 38, 111, 170n; forced removal of children from, 6, 17, 95–99; rape in Aboriginal communities, 102; Reconciliation with, xvi, 94–99; reintegrative shaming, 91–92; tradition of setting up camp, 68; and white shame, 45–47, 69–71, 94–106, 178n. *See also* Uluru
Abraham, Nicolas, 107
Abu-Lughod, Lila, 61–62
academics, 49, 131, 132–37, 139
Affect, Imagery, Consciousness (Tomkins), 18
affect scripts, 23, 24, 83–84
affects: as amplification, 20, 23, 110; as analog systems, 21; of behavioral data, 134–35;

and the body, 140–43; as collision of mind and body, 147; in concentration camps, 160; contrasted with cognition, 78; distinguished from emotions, xv, 11, 25–27, 66, 72, 172n; and face wrinkles, 18–19; hues of intensity of, 19–20; LaCapra on, 124; Nathanson's theory of affective experience, 66; objects of, 19; Tomkins on, 19–20, 22–23, 24–25, 27, 71, 83–84; treatises on, 136. *See also* emotions
Afghanistan, 89
aie, 123
alcoholism, 68
Alexander, Irving, 18, 24
Allen, Paula Gunn, 103–4
analogical operations, 19
Anangu people, 42
ancestral shame, xvii, 107–27
anger, xiii, 19, 22, 32, 70, 83, 98
anguish, 22
animals: shame in, 13

48; genetic structuralism
of, 48; on the habitus, xvi, 39,
48–56, 59, 61, 70, 72, 84;
on the researcher's relation
to the world, 51; response to
accusations of dogmatism,
50; on the social and the
body, 47–50; as a sociologist,
50, 51
boys, 91
brain, the, 65, 80–81
Braithwaite, John, xvi, 88–93,
106
*Bringing Them Home: The Report
of the National Inquiry into
the Separation of Aboriginal
and Torres Strait Islander
Children from their Families,*
95, 100
British Columbia, Canada, 112
British Intelligence Service, 145
Brown, Wendy, 77, 106
Buchenwald, 154

Camus, Albert, 4–5
Canada, 112
Capra, Robert, 82
"Caribou Trail The," (song), 118
Catalyst (television program),
80–81
celebrities, 165n
chemistry, 159
chiasmus, 122
children, 66, 121
China, 88
civil rights movement, 77
Clarke, Elspeth Honeyman,
115–20, 123–26

class, 50, 55, 62–63, 83
class shame, 120
cognition: contrasted with
affects, 78
collaborators, 82–83
colonialism, 109, 113, 122, 125
communication, 58, 150, 157
Communists, 151
concentration camps, 150–54,
157–58, 160–61
conditions of possibility, 12
conferencing movement, 89–90
Connolly, William, 35, 142
conservatism, 6
contact zones, xvii, 112–15, 122,
124, 127
contempt, 3, 22
Copernicus, 133
courage, 58
Craft for a Dry Lake (Mahood),
66–70
Crime, Shame, and Reintegration
(Braithwaite), 88
criminology, 88
cultural capital, 64, 172n
cultural theory, 12, 16, 164n
Cunneen, Chris, 100–101
Curie, Marie, 133
cybernetics, 19

Darwin, Charles, 13, 28, 29, 45,
129, 133
Deleuze, Gilles: on affect, 26;
on the body, 141, 142; on
ethology, 159; on T. E. Lawrence, 143–44, 146–49, 155;
notion of rhizome, 109; on
the process of feeling, 142;

Sedgwick, Eve K.: on affects,
19, 21–22, 28; aphorism
on people, 98; on cultural
theory, 16–17; on effect of
reading Tomkins, 140; on
ignorance, 100, 106; on
interest, 14; on physiological
expression of shame, 64; on
shame, 84–85; on Tomkins's
work on shame, 13–14; on
treatises on affects, 136;
writing of, 136
Semprun, Jorge, 154
sensation and perception, 26
Seven Pillars of Wisdom (Lawrence), 143
sex drive, 19
sexuality, x, 69, 86–87, 133
Shadows (artwork), 107–8
shame: acknowledgment of,
xii–xiv; as an affect of proximity, 34; ancestral shame,
xvii, 107–27; anthropology
of, 29–34; of being human,
152, 154–55; of being-out-
of-place, xvi, 38, 44–45, 62,
64–65, 66–70, 72; about
bodies, 27, 62–63, 160;
bodily expression of, 40, 53,
64, 71, 137; compared with
guilt, 2, 45–46; in con-
centration camps, 160–61;
contrasted with empathy,
105–6; controversy caused
by, 28; Deleuze on, 152;
denial of, 46; differing inten-
sities of, 14–15; etymological
origins, 131, 168n; genesis

of in the body, 27–28, 34,
146, 148; and glory, 143;
as hauntology, 124; Hegel
on, 2–3; as human, 152;
and humiliation, 22, 70; in
inability to convey interest,
130, 162; intergenerational
shame, 120, 121–22; King
on, 139; lack of, 32–33;
Lawrence on, 144, 146–49;
Lewis's model of, 27; in love,
ix–xii; to manage antisocial
behavior, xvi; in Melanesia,
30–31; objects of, 19; Piers
on, 3; political dimension of,
79; potentially transforming
effect of, 64; public declarations of, 94–100, 101, 105;
as punishment, xvi, 88–94;
recollections of, 1–2; relation
to gender, 77–87; relation
to interest, ix–xii, 13–15,
63–64, 71, 72; Rosaldo on,
169n; sharing to allevi-
ate pain of, 103–4; social
dimension of, 77, 83; social
management of, 31–32;
subjectivity of, 148; Tomkins
on, ix–xii, 13–14, 24, 28, 47,
124, 166n; whether affect
or emotion, 25–26; white
shame, 45–47, 69–71, 76,
94–106, 178n; in working-
class women, 62–63; writ-
ing shame, 130–32, 139,
147–48, 150, 158, 162, 171n
Shame and Its Sisters (Tomkins),
18

ELSPETH PROBYN is professor and chair of gender studies at the University of Sydney. Her previous books include *Sexing the Self: Gendered Positions in Cultural Studies, Outside Belongings, Carnal Appetites: FoodSexIdentities,* and *Sexy Bodies: The Strange Carnalities of Feminism.*